After The Guns Fall Silent:

The Enduring Legacy of Landmines

After The Guns Fall Silent:

The Enduring Legacy of Landmines

Shawn Roberts and Jody Williams

First Edition

Vietnam Veterans of America Foundation

Library of Congress Cataloging-in-Publication Data

Roberts, Shawn and Jody Williams
    After The Guns Fall Silent: The Enduring Legacy of Landmines
    Williams, Jody and Shawn Roberts,--First Edition
    Includes appendices, maps, and bibliography

Published by: Vietnam Veterans of America Foundation
    2001 S. Street, NW, Suite 740
    Washington, D.C. 20009

Distributed throughout the world by:
Oxfam UK and Ireland
274 Banbury Road
Oxford, OX2 7DZ
United Kingdom
(registered as a charity, no. 202918)

After The Guns Fall Silent: The Enduring Legacy of Landmines
is distributed by Oxfam UK and Ireland as a contribution to debate
on and understanding of the effects of landmines on communities
around the world, and their implications for international peace and
development. The authors and VVAF are entirely responsible for
the opinions expressed in this book.

ISBN 0 85598 337 X

9 780855 983376 >

Contents

Preface

A threat haunts Africa. It is the threat of millions of landmines contaminating almost one-third of the countries of Africa. Every day landmines affect the lives of African children. If they are not the victims of landmines themselves, their lives are forever changed when a parent becomes a mine casualty. Even when landmines do not claim victims directly, they have other ways of affecting people--such as depriving families of land to grow food or to graze their animals.

Recognizing that this threat exists--not only in Africa but in many countries throughout the world --the United Nations has called for the eventual elimination of landmines. People everywhere are beginning to seriously assess the impact of landmines and other weapons on children and civilian populations. Armed conflicts, and the indiscriminate or particularly injurious weapons used to wage them, are not the means to resolve socio-economic or political problems.

Africa is the most mined continent in the world. But it is not the only mined continent in the world. Millions of landmines can be found in 64 countries. As the Chairperson of the United Nations' Study on the Impact of Armed Conflict on Children, I have traveled widely to assess how war and the instruments of war affect children and their families. I have seen children victims of landmines and learned of the profound impact that landmines have on their lives.

Families all over the planet today experience the horrors of war. In the countries where countless numbers of landmines have been used in battle, those horrors will continue for decades. The millions of landmines sown throughout the world will continue to make victims of children and their families in countries where the wars are long silent.

Vietnam Veterans of America Foundation has been instrumental in raising awareness of the need to alleviate the civilian suffering caused by the proliferation of landmines. With this report, which documents the long-term impact of landmines on countries already devastated by decades of war, VVAF continues to contribute to the growing understanding of the implications of the continued use of landmines. It argues convincingly that the long-term cost of landmines outweighs their military usefulness and that the world will be a better place when it reaches its goal of eliminating landmines.

More must be done to eliminate the landmine threat that haunts so many countries of the world. The various sectors of civil society, governments and individuals everywhere must work together to eliminate that threat. This report helps us to understand what will happen in future wars if we are not successful.

Graça Machel
Chairperson

Acknowledgements

The research for *After The Guns Fall Silent: The Enduring Legacy of Landmines* was conducted by Vietnam Veterans of America Foundation with financial support from:

American Friends Service Committee/Cambodia
American Refugee Committee
Caritas - Germany
Joiner Center, University of Massachusetts
J. Roderick MacArthur Foundation
The John D. and Catherine T. MacArthur Foundation
Food and Agriculture Organization (FAO)/Afghanistan
Lutheran World Federation
Oxfam America
Oxfam Cambodia (for translating the report into Khmer)
Ploughshares Fund
Radda Barnen (Swedish Save the Children)
Swedish International Development Agency (SIDA)
R.F. Foundation
Ruth Mott Fund
Save the Children/U.S. (for the Afghanistan survey)
Samuel Rubin Foundation
The Schiebel Corporation
UN Department of Humanitarian Affairs
UNHCR/Afghanistan
UNICEF/Office of Emergency Programmes
UNICEF/Afghanistan
UNICEF/Cambodia
UNICEF/Emergency Operations in the former Yugoslavia
UN Office for the Coordination of Humanitarian Assistance to Afghanistan (UNOCHA)
United States Agency for International Development
World Vision International

We would like to thank the following people for their help with in-country research and village-level landmine surveys. In Afghanistan: Sayed Aqa, Mine Clearance Planning Agency; Ian Mansfield, UNOCHA Mines Clearance Programme; and A.W. Adil. Thanks to Gary Helseth, Save the Children US in Pakistan/Afghanistan and Bob Eaton. In Cambodia, Margo de Monchy of UNICEF and Chris Horwood of MAG. In Mozambique: Dr. Valeria Magni, the Mozambican Ministries of Health and Planning, and Jack McCarthy and Enrique Portillo. Ricky Weiss and Toni Strasburg also provided assistance. In the former Yugoslavia, research was made possible by the office of UNICEF/ Emergency Operations. Anne Nixon, Save the Children US, provided insights at formative stages of the research and Stephen Commins, World Vision International, has been an asset. Additional assistance for data analysis came from Vera Dolan, Herb and Louise Spirer, Doug Samuelson, Tom and Miney Jabine, Fritz Scheuren and Jim Vermillion, USAID. Carl von Essen and Radda Barnen supplied an insightful analysis of the draft of the report. Natalee Ernstrom, Andrew Bartlett, Stuart Maslen, Loren Stein, David Gould, and Susana Belovari provided research and editorial support. Mark Perry and Hank Poli edited the final report. Jasmine Desclaux provided the maps. Two people deserve specific thanks: Barbara Reed for her work on the village-level surveys in Cambodia and Afghanistan, and Helen Long for her work in the case-study countries.

List of Countries with Landmine Incidents (1 = Most Severe)

AFRICA

(1)	(2)	(3)
Angola	Chad	Botswana
Ethiopia	Liberia	Djibouti
Egypt	Mauritania	Guinea-Bissau
Eritrea	Morocco	Libya
Mozambique	Rwanda	Malawi
Somalia	Zinbabwe	Namibia
Sudan		Senegal
		Sierra Leone
		South Africa
		Tunisia
		Uganda

LATIN AMERICA

(1)	(2)	(3)
El Salvador**	Falklands/Malvinas	Chile
Nicaragua	Guatemala	Colombia
	Honduras	Costa Rica
		Cuba
		Ecuador****
		Mexico
		Peru****

EAST ASIA/PACIFIC

(1)	(2)	(3)
Cambodia	Burma	Malaysia
Vietnam	Laos	Philippines
China		Thailand
		South Korea

SOUTH ASIA

(1)	(2)	(3)
Afghanistan	Sri Lanka	India
		Pakistan

NEAR EAST

(1)	(2)	(3)
Iraq	Iran	Jordan
Kuwait	Israel	Oman
	Lebanon	
	Syria	
	Yemen	

EUROPE

(1)	(2)	(3)
Bosnia/Herzegovina	Armenia	Austria
Croatia	Azerbaijan	Belarus
	Georgia	Belgium
	Tadjikstan	Bulgaria
		Cyprus
		Estonia
		Germany
		Greece
		Latvia
		Lithuania
		Luxembourg
		Moldova
		The Netherlands
		Poland
		Russia
		Serbia
		Slovenia
		Turkey
		Ukraine

**   El Salvador now reports that its landmines have all been cleared.

****   The degree of severity of the landmine problem in the border clashes between Peru and Ecuador is not clear.

Sources: US Dept. of State, *Hidden Killers 1993*, *Hidden Killers 1994*; United Nations, *Assistance in Mine Clearance: Report of the Secretary-General*, A/49/357, 20 September 1994.

List of Contributions for Mine Clearance *

DONOR	RECIPIENT COUNTRY	1989-1990	1990-1991	1991-1992	1992-1993	1993-1994	1994-1995	1995-1996
Australia	Afghanistan	$164,546	$768,600	500,000 AUD/ $342,466	200,000 AUD/ $138,279	400,000 AUD/ $274,800		
	Cambodia					2.0 M AUD	2.5 M AUD	$1.06M Trust Fund/ $1.75M Open Pledge
	Mozambique					350,000 AUD		
	Namibia	N/A						
Austria	Afghanistan			$180,000			$155,740	
	Cambodia						$46,000	
Canada	Afghanistan					$562,559	$361,323	
	Angola						$380,000/ 277,000	
	Cambodia						$747K/ $746K	$1.25M 889,566
Denmark	Cambodia				$400,000	$1.05M		
Finland	Afghanistan			$235,294	$227,635	$175,991	$326,278	
France	Afghanistan	$644288	$349,406					
	Cambodia			$600,000		1M ECU via EC		$838,600 /F4M to COFRAS
Ireland	Cambodia					300,000 Irish Pd.	425,000 Irish Pd.	425,000 Irish Pd.
	Mozambique						425,000 Irish Pd.	425,000 Irish Pd.
	Angola						425,000 Irish Pd.	425,000 Irish Pd.
	UN Trust Fund							$100,000
Italy	Mozambique						$843,013	

*Data was based on all sources of information made available to VVAF at the time of publication.

DONOR COUNTRY	RECIPIENT COUNTRY	1989-1990	1990-1991	1991-1992	1992-1993	1993-1994	1994-1995	1995-1996
Japan	Afghanistan	$5 M		$5 M		$2 M	$14 M	
	Cambodia						$2.5 M	
	Somalia						$0.2 M	
Korea, Rep.						$75,000		
Netherlands	Afghanistan			$284,091 + $84,929	$806,452	$329,670	$312,500	
	Angola							$1.9 M
	Cambodia						$1.04M	
	Iraq				$ 80,645	$53,308	$6,738	
	Laos							$218,750
	Mozambique						$2.5M	$1.25M
New Zealand	Cambodia					$250,000 /$139750	$50,000 /$8,313	/$37,004
	UN Trust Fund						$80,415 (MCPU)	$66,667 for 3 yrs.
Norway	Afghanistan	$14K			$1.9 M	$1.8 M		
	Angola					8.9 M NOK	20.0M NOK	
	Cambodia			6.8 M NOK	7.0 M NOK	14.0 M NOK	7.0 M NOK	
	N.Iraq/ Kurdistan						6.0 M NOK	
	Mozambique				6.0 M NOK	16.0M NOK	21.5M NOK	
	UN Trust Fund							$1.34 M
So. Africa	Angola						$163,000	

DONOR COUNTRY	RECIPIENT COUNTRY	1989-1990	1990-1991	1991-1992	1992-1993	1993-1994	1994-1995	1995-1996
Sweden (*$20 M total +$7M)	Afghanistan*			$898,457	$520,156	$1.15M		
	Angola*							
	Cambodia*						$2.1 M	
	Iraq*							
	Laos*							
	Mozambique*							
	Nicaragua*							
	General* (R&D)							$6.0 M
	UN Trust Fund*							$1.0 M
Switzerland	Afghanistan					$709,220		
	Angola							$438,596
	UN Trust Fund							$438,596
UK	Afghanistan				£1.2 M	£916,131	£1.2 M	£160,750
	Angola						£722,068 MAG £899,430 HALO £226,029 CMAO	£103,570 HALO
	Cambodia			£ 60,000	£206,337	£1.46 M	£1.69 M	£364,238
	N. Iraq					£200,439		
	Mozambique					£574,586	£414,832	
	Rwanda						£30,000	
	Somalia			£300,000	£373,540			
	Yemen						£100,000	
	UN Trust Fund						£500,000	$795,000 (MCPU)

DONOR COUNTRY	RECIPIENT COUNTRY	1989-1990	1990-1991	1991-1992	1992-1993	1993-1994	1994-1995	1995-1996
United States	Afghanistan	$10M				$1.5 M + $1.48 M	$500,000	$1 M cash + $2 M equip.
	Angola							$2 M equip.
	Cambodia						$750,000/ $710,189	$2.7 M/ $1.3 M
	Eritrea						$200,000	$2.7 M/ $460,000
	Ethiopia						$300,000	$2.1 M/ $300,000
	Laos							$80,000
	Mozambique						$400,000+ $5 M (Ronco)	$800,000
	Namibia						--	$270,000
	OAS/IADB						$350,000	$300,000 /200,000
	Rwanda						--	$4.5 M/ $300,000
	Somalia						N/A	N/A
	Unallocated							$1.17M

DONOR	RECIPIENT COUNTRY	1989-1990	1990-1991	1991-1992	1992-1993	1993-1994	1994-1995	1995-1996
European Comm.	Afghanistan				9.4 M ECUs	600,000 ECUs	500,000 ECUs	
	Cambodia				364,000 ECUs (HALO)	378,878 ECUs (HALO) 460,085 ECUs (MAG) 1 M ECUs (Cofras)	1.18 M ECUs (HALO and MAG)	
	Iraq				1.5 M ECUs (HI)	2.4 M ECUs (MAG)	1.0 M ECUs (MAG)	
	Mozambique				370,000 ECUs	1.53 M ECUs		
	Somalia				215,000 ECUs (MSF-Holland)	455,000 ECUs (MSF-Holland)		
OAS	Nicaragua				$ 2 M			
	Honduras and Costa Rica					$1.5 M		

Contributions of Personnel for Humanitarian Mine Clearance

DONOR COUNTRY	RECIPIENT COUNTRY	1989-90 No. of Personnel	1990-91 (No.)	1991-92 (No.)	1992-93 (No.)	1993-94 (No.)	1994-95 (No.)	1995-96 (No.)
Australia	Afghanistan	92	92	92	92	92		
	Cambodia					8	8	8
	Namibia	304						
Belgium	Cambodia					5	2	
Canada	Afghanistan	50						
	Angola						2	
	Cambodia					12	7	
France	Cambodia					1	1	
Netherlands	Angola							16
	Cambodia					2	2	
	Mozambique						11	
New Zealand	Afghanistan	30	30	30				
	Angola							12
	Cambodia			27	21	N/A	2	
	Mozambique					9	2	
United States	Cambodia						40	
	Honduras							7

Contributions for Demining Research and Development

Donor Country	Recipient	Date	Amount
Canada	Defence Research Establishment (Suffield)	1995	$6,000,000
United States	Department of Defense	1995	$10,000,000
United Kingdom	Defence Research Agency	1994-1995	£ 104,928

Part One

Executive Summary

Executive Summary

Landmines are called cheap weapons and in strictly military terms, they may well be. But in humanitarian terms, they are not. One hundred million landmines are found in 64 countries--most of them in the developing world. An additional 100 million landmines are stockpiled and ready for use. Landmines disrupt society and severely hamper post-conflict reconstruction. And they kill and maim thousands of people each year. There are already at least 250,000 landmine-disabled people in the world, and that number is growing.[1] Landmines continue to claim 500 victims a week--the equivalent of 26,000 new victims each and every year.[2]

Over 400 million landmines have been deployed since the beginning of World War II, including more than 65 million[3] in the 15 years since the formulation of the *1980 Convention on Conventional Weapons* (CCW)[4] which attempts to regulate their use. Afghanistan, Angola, Cambodia, Mozambique, Croatia, and Bosnia-Herzegovina are six of the most severely landmine-contaminated countries in the world. Almost one-third of the world's landmines are found in them. Throughout 1994 and early 1995, Vietnam Veterans of America Foundation (VVAF) conducted detailed research on the landmine problems of these nations. Thousands of households in Afghanistan, Cambodia, Bosnia-Herzegovina and Mozambique were interviewed for this report.[5] VVAF also carried out field missions to Angola and Croatia. *After The Guns Fall Silent: The Enduring Legacy of Landmines* is the result of that research.

I. A Global Problem

Landmines and Humanitarian Law

Perhaps the impact of landmines seems obvious. But the impact of landmines is far greater than the direct medical and rehabilitation costs for the world's landmine victims, which is now calculated at $750 million.[6] The effect of landmines is far in excess of the direct cost of clearing these lethal toxins from the soil--which will take decades of slow and painstaking work at a minimum cost of $33 billion dollars.[7] Landmines directly or indirectly affect almost every aspect of national life in mine-contaminated countries and the daily lives of those who live in them.

Researching the socio-economic cost of landmines is not simply an academic exercise; the laws of war seek to limit the effect of armed conflict on civilians. The basic tenets of humanitarian law dictate that there are limits to the means that soldiers may use to achieve their ends: there must be a balance between military needs and consequences to the civilian population. That balance is to be proportional. Humanitarian law states that soldiers and their weapons must discriminate between combatants and civilians, who are not to be targets in war. These two fundamental principles of humanitarian law--proportionality and discrimination--are to be applied whenever landmines are used. As part of customary law, these tenets apply to all states, regardless of other treaty obligations.

3

In addition, in recognition of the particularly injurious or indiscriminate nature of certain conventional weapons, attempts have been made to further restrict and codify their use through the CCW. Unfortunately, the CCW's Protocol II (the Landmines Protocol) has been ineffective in controlling the proliferation and indiscriminate use of landmines.

Proponents of landmine use focus on the utility and cost-effectiveness of the weapon. Landmines are called a "force-multiplier" whose effect magnifies the usefulness of other weapons. The proponents of landmine use argue that, when directed toward a military target, the collateral damage they cause can be controlled. In this limited battlefield scenario, the proportion of damage inflicted on civilians (it is argued) does not outweigh the overriding need of the military for landmines. In theory, the argument seems elegant--especially when it is rigorously confined to the impact of landmines during the period of the military engagement itself. But when the life-cycle of the weapon and its impact over generations are factored into the equation, the question of proportionality takes on new meaning.

Because the actual consequences of landmine use continue for decades after their initial deployment, their immediate battlefield utility is outweighed by the long-term costs to civilian populations. Over time (and in many cases during the time of engagement itself), landmines harm civilian populations and the environments in which they live to a far greater degree than the military targets at which they are aimed. The international negotiations on conventional weapons that began two decades ago did not take into account the life-cycle of landmines. Because the effect of landmines was only considered during military engagements, the CCW's formulation has made it ineffective in lessening the impact of landmines on civil society. Despite the growing body of information about the long-term impact of landmines, government meetings in 1994 and 1995 to prepare for review of the CCW in September 1995 have given minimal weight to the larger socio-economic implications of continued landmine use.

The military perspective is still accepted as the point of departure for negotiations on landmine use, and conventional military doctrine forms the framework of that discussion. Military doctrine incorporates landmines as one in an array of tools that shape the battlefield. Overwhelming weight is given to their use as a defensive weapon whose primary functions are to serve as a semi-permanent barrier and to obstruct enemy mobility. Used as a barrier, landmines protect national borders, military and economic assets, and fighting forces themselves. When used to obstruct enemy mobility, mines are laid to restrict the battle area and force deployment of enemy troops into areas where the defender is best able to defeat them. Landmines can cause delay and particular vulnerability while the enemy tries to breach the minefield. This can give defending forces time for redeployment and attack. When this doctrine is presented to civilian audiences in particular, emphasis is given to the defensive nature of the weapon, especially its utility in protecting one's own troops. The implication is that regular military forces use landmines for strictly defensive purposes-- and that the abrogation of humanitarian law (the use of landmines to target civilian populations) arises with irregular forces.

This study shows otherwise. In the countries investigated for this report, landmines have been used

4

by both regular and irregular forces, in direct contravention of international law. In all of these countries, landmines have been used to defend military and strategic assets. But they have also been used in far greater numbers as offensive weapons. Just as landmines have been used to deny access of terrain to enemy troops, they have been deployed to depopulate whole sections of countries, to disrupt agriculture, to interrupt transportation, to damage economic infrastructure, and to kill and maim thousands of innocent civilians. Landmines have been used by both regular and irregular armies to undermine the social and economic fabric of society. They have been deployed to make vital economic assets useless and cripple the economic and social redevelopment of these countries after the wars are over.

It is beyond the scope of this report to address the utility of landmines or their impact on military forces. However, it is important to note that some military officials have raised questions about landmine use which require further study. One former U.S. Marine Corps Commandant has stated: "I know of no situation in the Korean war, nor in the five years I served in Southeast Asia, nor in Panama, nor Desert Shield-Desert Storm where our use of mine warfare truly channelized the enemy and brought him into a destructive pattern ... I'm not aware of any operational advantage from [the] broad deployment of mines."[8] A recent study commissioned by the U.S. Department of Defense states that in order for the utility of landmines to preclude arms control considerations, an especially demanding set of assumptions must be made--particularly for antipersonnel landmines. The study concludes: "It is far from obvious that the required assumptions can be sustained."[9] The assertion that landmines are necessary for troop protection also bears investigation. The limited information on this subject shows that in 1965, in the midst of the Vietnam War, between 65 and 70 percent Marine Corps casualties resulted from landmines and booby traps.[10] That is a high number, but it is not unusual. In 1970, during the Angolan war for independence, fifty percent of all Portuguese casualties were attributed to landmines.[11]

Many kinds of antipersonnel landmines are designed specifically to maim, a tactic that is deliberately designed to overload an enemy's logistical system. Most mine victims require more extensive medical treatment than other kinds of casualties, thus taking up valuable resources. But landmines do not discriminate between the military and society as a whole. As a result, the impact of landmines on the minimal health care systems of the countries where they have been used in great numbers has been overwhelming. The psychological impact of landmine use on an enemy is undeniable (the shock wave of a mine blast can freeze an army patrol in its tracks), but landmines also terrorize and demoralize civil society. Put simply, anything that landmines can do to an enemy's army, they can also do to a civilian population. What they cannot do is discriminate between the soldier and the civilian.

The Social and Economic Costs of Landmines

Because landmines cannot discriminate, because their destructive capacity does not end with the signing of a peace agreement, the long-term socio-economic cost of landmines dwarfs their immediate military usefulness. The millions of landmines sown in the world today are prolonging the effects of wars long decided. Landmines sown in World War Two still kill and maim today in

Europe and North Africa. Landmines still deny the use of large areas of land and continue to cause casualties in Vietnam--twenty years after America's withdrawal from Southeast Asia. Unlike other weapons of war, landmines--and other explosive devices that act like landmines[12] --continue to kill and maim long after the guns of war are silent.

Large portions of the national territories of the countries focused on in this report have been--or still are--battlegrounds. Large numbers of these battlegrounds are agricultural and grazing lands. The mining of these lands has led to increased poverty. Farmers and nomadic populations have been forced to abandon rural areas and attempt to adjust to life in urban environments. Even in cases where large tracts of agricultural land have not been mined, irrigation systems and wells often have been--making it difficult or impossible to farm or maintain herds. But the agricultural base of these agrarian societies has not been the only target of landmines.

Countries with a minimal infrastructure (like those studied in this report) are particularly vulnerable to landmine use. Dams and electrical installations have been mined, which can seriously reduce the ability of a nation to produce the power necessary for reconstruction. Transportation systems have been mined, interrupting the movement of people and the flow of goods and services. Market systems have been seriously disrupted or abandoned because farmers and herders have been unable to move over mined roads and footpaths to bring their produce to market. Such disruption has a direct impact on employment, and rising prices for goods and services (made scarce by such restricted movement) contributes to inflation. Landmines have also magnified the effect of droughts, because mine-contaminated roads have impeded the movement of domestic foodstuffs and hampered food relief.

When this complex interplay of social and economic factors results in the inability of people to meet their own needs, they have become an economic burden on the global community. In 1993, United Nations' appeals for humanitarian assistance for 16 countries totalled $2.5 billion. Thirteen of those countries have serious mine problems.[13] Unless and until landmines are cleared, it is difficult for life to return to normal and for people to begin to rebuild their lives. Yet most mine-contaminated countries do not have the ability to fund mine clearance. They must rely on financial assistance from the international community to develop and sustain demining programs. Kuwait is the only severely mined country that has the resources to finance its own mine clearance operations.[14]

Demining

While many are familiar with military minefield breaching, the concept of humanitarian mine clearance has developed only recently as the extent of landmine contamination has become apparent with the end of the Cold War. Breaching can be accomplished by various methods, but the essential goal is to cut a path to move troops and equipment through a minefield. Mines outside the path are disregarded, and a lower mine clearance rate is tolerated because soldiers expect to take casualties. But humanitarian mine clearance involves the removal of all mines--the United Nations standard is 99.9 percent--to return previously mined land to its pre-war condition.

The United Nations' first attempts at developing humanitarian clearance capabilities in host countries reflected a lack of clarity about the breadth and nature of the landmine problem, and how best to solve it. Within the UN bureaucracy, there was reluctance to take on long-term clearance operations, a reluctance that manifested itself in concerns about "liability" and "mandate." If responsibility for mine clearance rested with the contaminated country, then international responsibility was minimal--if it existed at all. Demining programs were, therefore, to be organized, controlled, and carried out domestically. The UN would train indigenous personnel, but the actual demining was to be left in their hands. This conception of mine clearance resulted in problems: deminers were sometimes trained without the establishment of a clearance program that could put their training to use. In some cases, demining priorities were set before the extent of the landmine problem was adequately assessed. In other cases, sophisticated equipment was brought into countries that was not appropriate to the local environment. While the United Nations developed impressive programs in some countries--such as in Afghanistan and Cambodia--the establishment of new programs in host countries has frequently repeated old patterns.

The development of new technologies to make mine clearance more rapid faces huge obstacles. Mine detection equipment developed in the 1940s is still being used to counter landmines developed in the 1980s and 1990s. Mines that were once made of metal (and are relatively easy to detect) are now made of plastic, a material that cannot be detected through the use of four-decade-old technology. In Cambodia, for example, for every mine found, an average of 129 harmless metal fragments are detected;[15] each instance of possible mine contamination must be investigated. In addition, mines have become sophisticated weapons systems with electronic fuses and sensors that make them even more deadly. Such mines can sense foot-step patterns and body heat, and even the signal of a mine detector--all or any of which can make them explode.

An assessment of landmines by the US military recognizes that the "explosion of technological sophistication in landmines presents keen challenges" to developing countermine programs. The assessment notes that the costs of most improvements to landmines are much less expensive than the technologies needed to counter them. The report concludes: "Each landmine technology may be easily countered when faced alone. As a result, many landmine developers are incorporating several technologies into each landmine. Forces must be equipped with countermine assets capable of defeating all the valid threats simultaneously. This may mean fielding multiple countermine systems to ensure the total landmine threat is adequately addressed."[16] Such sophistication is--and likely will remain--beyond the reach of most mine-contaminated countries.

Clearance is made even more difficult by an almost complete disregard for minefield mapping. Military doctrine instructs in the mapping and recording of minefields. And while the CCW requires the mapping of "pre-planned" minefields; just what the term "pre-planned" means is not defined. But even if it were, it is likely the definition would not be followed. As the United Nations and other experts involved in humanitarian mine clearance have repeatedly stated, minefields are rarely mapped or recorded. Additionally, advances in mine delivery systems make it possible to remotely scatter mines at rates of well over 1000 per minute.[17] While it might be possible to record the general location of remotely-delivered mines, the military itself concedes that accurate mapping of such minefields is impossible.[18]

In heavily contested areas, which can be found in all the countries in this report, minefields are often sown on top of each other, so that even when maps have been made, they do not record all of the new mines that have been laid. The situation is complicated when battle fronts shift over an area and opposing forces mine and remine to defend their respective positions. Weather conditions also can shift mine positions. In some instances, mines sown on riverbanks have been washed downstream, while mines sown in deserts move easily and frequently in shifting sands.

The sheer number of landmines requiring clearance is overwhelming; but the numbers alone do not adequately explain the problem. It takes 100 times as long to remove a landmine as to deploy it. A field with one landmine in it can be removed from productive use as surely as a field with 100 landmines, and it can take a mine clearance team as long to demine a field with one mine in it as a field with 100 mines. The process for determining whether a field is mined or not is the same. Where there is fear of mine contamination the entire area must be painstakingly combed and probed, either to remove actual mines--or to prove that none exist. If no more mines were deployed from this day forward, it would still take decades to clear the earth of this lethal and indiscriminate weapon.

Because it is impossible to clear all landmines from mine contaminated countries even in the medium term, clearance programs have prioritized demining operations. Criteria for prioritization vary from program to program. To attempt to minimize casualties while mine contamination is brought under control, clearance programs incorporate mine awareness training for local populations. Mine awareness programs target refugee and displaced populations in particular, since they are at particular risk from landmines. Additionally, UN agencies and NGOs have begun awareness programs to target specific populations. Mine awareness programs have continued to develop with the increasing understanding of how landmines affect populations, but it is important to note that even where mine awareness training has been carried out, people will enter known mined areas when they have no economic option.

The Human Cost

The victims of landmines are almost inevitably the poorest and most vulnerable members of society. It is the subsistence farmer, nomads and their herds, and fleeing refugees and the displaced who are most often affected. Economic necessity--bare survival--forces people to enter known mined areas in search of food and water, to graze livestock, to grow food, cut wood, or gather thatch to sell or for building materials. Moreover, those people who live and work among landmines are very often the same people who rely most on their physical fitness for work and who can least afford the care necessary to treat landmine injuries.

Landmines maim and kill. The percentage of those killed by a landmine blast varies from country to country, but in all cases the numbers are significant. The International Committee of the Red Cross (ICRC) surgical database begun in 1991 has recorded 23,767 war-wounded patients treated for landmine injuries in their facilities in Pakistan, on the Thai-Cambodia border, and on the

Sudanese border with Kenya. The ICRC's data reflects a hospital mortality rate of 3.7 percent.[19] Survey results at the household level for this report show a death rate of 31 percent in Cambodia, and 59 percent in Afghanistan. In other words, this study shows that most of those who die from landmine blasts do not make it to a medical facility.

The overwhelming majority of mine victims are adult males. There was considerable concern that the lower percentage of women and children victims was a false indicator of the degree of the problem. It was hypothesized that women and children are statistically under represented because they die from their wounds without making it to medical facilities, or because they are denied access to rehabilitation programs. In the populations surveyed for this report, these hypotheses were not borne out.

Because many landmines are designed to maim their victims, the kinds of wounds they cause often require extensive treatment for long periods of time. The medical and rehabilitative costs stemming from landmine casualties result in significant economic burden to both the nation and to mine victims and their families. The first aid administered to mine victims is often rudimentary; in some cases inappropriately applied tourniquets result in amputations that otherwise might not have been necessary. Another significant obstacle victims face is the lack of transportation, which is coupled to the fact that medical facilities generally are long distances from the location of landmine incidents. The number of hours it takes to reach medical care can make a significant difference in the extent of amputation necessary and in the subsequent likelihood of infection. This, in turn, affects the length of treatment, the consumption of hospital resources, and the drain on family resources. Delays beyond six hours in reaching care significantly increase the probability of infection. Current statistics show that the vast majority of victims do not make it to medical facilities within that six-hour period.

Landmine-contaminated countries do not have the medical infrastructure to respond to the needs of landmine victims. The majority of facilities are ill-equipped to deal with landmine injuries and often unnecessary loss of limb and life results not only from poor medical facilities with unsanitary conditions, but also because of inexpert surgical skill. More critically, modern antipersonnel mines inflict much more severe injuries than wounds made by other conventional weapons. Because this is only recently understood, most medical personnel have not been trained in the surgical techniques necessary to adequately treat landmine injuries. However, the number of mine victims is not the only factor to consider in determining the overall cost of landmine injuries. Mine injuries require a disproportionate amount of medical resources compared to other war-related injuries and especially when compared to typical, non-war-related surgeries.

The impact of the mine explosion extends far beyond the individual casualty. From the moment of an incident, others are involved in evacuation and emergency care, in transport to the hospital, in surgery and post-operative treatment, and in rehabilitation services and vocational training. In most instances a family member must not only accompany the victim to the hospital, but also stay there to ensure that food and other basic needs are met. In countries investigated for this report, families reported having to spend an amount equivalent of up to two-and-one-half times their annual income on immediate costs related to the mine injuries.

Landmines and Children

Recently, the UN Secretary General commissioned a study of the impact of armed conflict on children. The study was specifically instructed to consider means of protecting children from "indiscriminate use of all weapons of war, especially antipersonnel mines."[20] There is now little doubt that landmines have a particularly egregious impact on the young. While casualty rates for child victims of landmines differ significantly between countries, the ways in which landmines affect children everywhere are the same. Children are vulnerable to antipersonnel mines simply because they are children--because of their size and their natural curiosity. Children are often too small to see mines that are clearly visible to adults. Unable to keep up with adults traveling by foot, children may stray off safe routes into minefields, may not recognize minefield warning signs, or may not be able to read written warnings at all. In many cultures, children are required to perform tasks critical to the survival of the family, such as herding animals, collecting water or firewood, or scavenging. In areas that have been extensively mined, these activities expose children to grave risks.

While there is no evidence that landmines are designed like toys to attract children, children are attracted to landmines because they are easily attracted by unknown objects. The results can be deadly. Children in heavily mined areas may become so familiar with mines that they forget they are lethal weapons, a reversal, as one mine expert has noted, of "the common perception of the 'hidden mine.'" In northern Iraq, "rural children commonly use mines as wheels for toy trucks and go-carts; in Cambodia they play boules with B40 anti-personnel mines." Even where children recognize the danger of mines, "there can not be an automatic assumption that such knowledge will deter them from tampering with mines. Especially among young boys, the risk element itself may prove a fatal attraction. In Afghanistan they compete in throwing stones at PFM-1 'Butterfly' mines, the winner being the child whose stone causes the mine to detonate; similar behavior has been observed in other mined regions."[21]

Landmine injuries more often than not require multiple surgeries, which are particularly traumatic to children. In addition, as the child develops, the bone of the amputation site grows more than surrounding tissue and can require reamputation, sometimes repeatedly. Children also need new prostheses repeatedly as they grow. While the prosthetic devices themselves may be provided by international relief agencies, often the time away from home--both for the child and for the adult care giver--required for making and fitting a new prosthesis places an undue burden on the family and makes such ongoing care impossible. Not only are the young victims a drain on scarce resources, but they also may no longer be able to contribute to the family which can have a profound psychological impact on the child and on the family as a whole.

Landmines also have an effect on children when their parents are mine victims. Loss of employment and resulting impact on food security directly affects children. In some cases, children have had to leave school when their parents have fallen victim to landmines either to accompany the parent to the hospital or to work to try to supplement the now-reduced family income. Landmines also have had an impact on family food security, and thus the nutrition of children, where the degree of mine contamination has made it impossible for families to cultivate food or has reduced the amount of land available for farming or raising livestock.

Landmines and the Displaced

There are specific ways in which refugees and internally displaced persons (IDPs) are particularly affected by landmines. In some cases, landmines cause displacement, while in others, landmines inhibit the return home or make life difficult after a return. The existence of landmines is often but one factor in decisions to return home. Generally, it is the over-all security situation, including the prospect of political stability, that discourages return. Even so, while people will avoid returning to heavily-mined areas (such as the Mutarara District of Mozambique's Tete Province and the area around Jalalabad City in Afghanistan), they have also returned to them in large numbers--as graphically illustrated in Kabul, Afghanistan in early 1995, and in those areas of Cambodia declared as "no-go" zones by the United Nations High Commissioner for Refugees.

Mined transportation systems can impede and endanger repatriation and resettlement. But even when mined roads are cleared, problems continue. While populations that have not been displaced by fighting are sometimes more aware of locations of minefields, returning refugee populations and IDPs are not. When these populations return home, sharp increases in mine casualties are seen. In many instances, displaced persons return home to find that the most productive and mine-free lands have been occupied by families who did not leave during the fighting. Competition for mine-free land can exacerbate other post-conflict pressures and threaten peace. In addition, where fear of landmines and generalized instability have impeded refugee resettlement, the prolonged stay of such populations in countries of exile can place undue burdens on the host country--and on international relief efforts. Such long-term displacement can also put strains on regional stability.

The Environment

Where landmines have been used in large numbers, they have had a significant effect on already taxed environments. Populations with mine-limited access to agricultural or grazing land are pushed onto increasingly fragile, marginal lands, furthering the land's rapid degradation. In some instances, where water resources have been mined, traditional rangelands have been affected, causing over-exploitation of fragile areas. Where mine contamination has reached a degree which disrupts traditional rural lifestyles, such populations may be forced to move into urban environments, thereby contributing to overcrowding, unemployment and other urban problems.

Deforestation has been accelerated by extensive use of landmines. Where arable land has been mined to such a degree that forests become the only source of livelihood, the long-term consequences of selling old forests and fruit trees give way to immediate survival pressures. Deforestation can, in turn, affect marshlands and watertables, which have an impact on fish and other wildlife. Landmines have also threatened the already fragile environments of some rare animals, such as the snow leopard in Afghanistan--which is already in danger of extinction. In Africa, elephants and other animals have been killed or maimed by landmines after national parks have been used as military bases. One of the few remaining male silver-backed gorillas fell victim to landmines.

II. Country Case Studies

Afghanistan

Afghanistan has experienced political upheaval since 1973 and open war, *jihad* (holy war), since 1978. The Soviet Union invaded the country on Christmas Eve 1979 to support the faltering regime and occupied Afghanistan until February 1989, when Soviet forces withdrew. Fighting did not end with the Soviet withdrawal and subsequent collapse of the government. Intense factional fighting continues to this day.

All sides in the conflict have used mines, but the vast majority were laid by Soviet or regime forces who used protective minefields extensively around military posts and vital assets, such as airports, government installations and power stations. Major cities such as Herat, Kandahar, Jalalabad and Khost were also mined. Soviet forces dropped scatterable "butterfly"[22] mines indiscriminately by the millions on mountain passes, villages and enemy bases.[23] The *mujahedeen* used far fewer mines, (primarily antitank mines) on roads and tracks to block enemy deployments and support ambushes. New mines have been laid in 1994 and early 1995 in the continuing fighting.

The ten million landmines in Afghanistan are scattered through 27 of the country's 29 provinces. In some regions of the country, mines are found nearly everywhere. In other areas a few mines deny the use of vast areas of land. As of early 1995, 4235 minefields, including 252 minefields newly identified in Kabul city in 1995, affected 488.9 square kilometers of the country. The western, southern and eastern provinces bordering Iran and Pakistan are the most heavily mined. Landmine contamination is so severe that until mines are cleared from priority areas, major rehabilitation and reconstruction activities cannot take place.

Approximately 90 percent of the 4235 minefields identified in Afghanistan have been found in agricultural lands and grazing land and--to a lesser extent--in or near irrigation systems. During the Soviet occupation, the rural areas of the country believed to support the *mujahedeen* were depopulated through bombing and extensive mining of villages and rural areas. This policy resulted in the displacement of two million farmers. The corresponding drop in food production and increased demand on the part of the displaced contributed to an inflation rate of 200 to 300 percent for food and fuel.[24] Of the total mined area in Afghanistan, approximately 25 percent is agricultural land. By 1994, only a little more than one-fifth of that land had been cleared. Mined grazing land represents almost two-thirds of the total mined land in the country. Approximately four percent of that total was cleared by the end of 1994.

Landmines either block the use of the land directly or because of mined irrigation systems. The mining of water systems has had a profound affect on daily agricultural life in the country. Once destroyed or encircled by mines, depriving people of water for crops, for their animals and for themselves, their loss can ruin the economy of a village. The mining of water sources in Afghanistan has had a particularly significant impact because three-quarters of all wheat production in the country and 85 percent of food and agricultural crops are grown on irrigated land.

In Afghanistan, 66,602 people were surveyed for this report. Families from rural villages in six provinces, from refugee camps in Pakistan and camps for the displaced inside Afghanistan, and representing *kuchi* nomads were interviewed.[25] The responses of these 8699 households give a clear picture of the effect of landmines on the lives of the people of Afghanistan.

In the rural villages surveyed, the food production of forty-three percent of the families interviewed was affected by landmines. Landmine contamination prevents the cultivation of additional land totalling 150 percent of the agricultural land currently under cultivation. Eighty percent of the families surveyed found landmines in their fields, barring cultivation. Mined irrigation systems reduced available land for another 16 percent of the families interviewed. Families have also lost significant numbers of their livestock (a primary asset), to landmines. At least 60 percent of all cattle and 40 percent of all sheep and goats in Afghanistan have been lost or killed in the war. More than one-third of the 4990 village households interviewed had lost at least one animal; forty-seven percent of the flocks owned by these rural villagers were lost to landmines. The direct loss to these families, not considering the lost productivity of the animals, is $3,393,473.[26] Additionally, 38 percent of the refugee families interviewed in Pakistan reported having lost a number equal to 50 percent of their current livestock holdings.

The impact of landmines on the *kuchi* nomads of Afghanistan has been particularly devastating. The dissemination of landmines across traditional *kuchi* grazing lands and migration routes has had a significant impact on migratory patterns, which has often brought the *kuchi* into conflict with villagers over grazing rights. The long-term impact on the *kuchi* culture can be seen in the numbers of groups who have abandoned their traditional way of life and live either as refugees or barely survive on scarce jobs.[27] Sixty-five percent of *kuchi* nomads interviewed for this report had lost at least one animal to landmines. The 34,394 animals killed is equal to 60 percent of current flocks owned by the 1432 families surveyed, representing a direct loss to the *kuchi* families of $2,841,236. While *kuchi* households represented 16.4 percent of the families interviewed, their loss of livestock was 45.5 percent of the total reported in the survey. Overall 53 percent of *kuchi* landmine victims were injured while tending their animals; 44 percent of women and 60 percent of *kuchi* children mine victims were tending animals when injured.

In Afghanistan, the production of wheat and other principal foods is concentrated in different parts of the country. The distribution of food from surplus to deficit areas has been significantly affected by mined transportation routes. In 1992 it was estimated that road freight had declined from 1943 to 1080 million tons per kilometer.[28] This disruption has contributed to the rapid inflation of food prices. Minefields were found in 521 stretches of road in Afghanistan. By mid-1995, 327 of these mined areas affecting 22 provinces were still awaiting mine clearance.[29] The direct cost for that demining will be approximately $4 million. Although mine clearance costs vary significantly depending on weather, terrain, general road conditions, the presence of ordnance and density of mines, the average cost of demining per kilometer of road in Afghanistan is $15,000 ($.80 per sq meter).

Afghanistan's electrical production system has also been extensively mined. The largest dam in the country, Kajakai Dam, did not produce electricity for nearly a decade because of landmines. Electrical pylons have also been mined, especially those linking the Kajakai with Kandahar City and the Sarobi Dam with Kabul. Some pylons around the Sarobi Dam have been cleared and remaining pylons are included as priority areas for clearance.

Afghanistan's urban centers have also been affected by mines. Herat is ringed by huge minefields. Residential areas in and around Herat were also heavily mined, which has discouraged rebuilding. The fierce fighting for control of Kabul has resulted in the virtual destruction of the city. After a lull in fighting in the city in March 1995, 252 minefields were newly identified, affecting over 22 sq km of land. The rubble of Kabul conceals thousands of landmines, making rebuilding of the city and its infrastructure a deadly prospect. In the first three weeks of April 1995 alone, 1500 people trying to reclaim their homes and their livelihoods fell victim to landmines in Kabul. Jalalabad in Nangarhar province, which has become a refuge for tens of thousands displaced by the fighting in Kabul, has also been ringed by minefields.

An assessment of the mine problem at the time of the Soviet withdrawal from Afghanistan led the United Nations to develop a demining program as part of its short-term reconstruction plan for the country. The first foreign military teams arrived in February 1989 to assist UNOCA in setting up centers to train Afghans in minefield surveying and demining. The initial objective of the program was to train as many Afghan refugees as possible in mine awareness and 13,000 men in basic mine clearance to then clear their home villages. It quickly became evident, however, that unsupervised local mine clearance would not work. The program was reorganized in 1990 to establish trained and organized Afghan mine clearance teams capable of operation anywhere in Afghanistan. The first organized UN demining operation began in January 1990 with one 24-man Afghan team with expatriate advisors and supervisors. By 1995, the UN Mine Clearance Program employed almost 3000 Afghan deminers and support personnel. The program operates with 48 clearance teams, 20 survey teams, 34 dog teams, and 16 mine awareness teams. Its annual budget is $25 million.

The Mine Clearance Program emphasizes clearance of high priority areas for economic and agricultural development. Of the 4235 minefields that have been surveyed, covering 488.9 sq km of land, 118.1 sq km have been designated as high priority for clearance. By the end of 1994, 54.3 sq km had been cleared and the remaining high priority areas were projected to be finished by late 1997.[30] The current rate of clearance is 20 sq km annually. The program plans to survey and mark an additional 18 sq km of high priority area during 1995. Seventy-five percent of mined land falls outside the high priority criteria for clearance. Additionally, between January 1990 and December 1994, almost two million Afghans received mine awareness education. Awareness programs focus on mine identification, mine avoidance techniques, and what to do in the event of injury.

There have been hundreds of thousands of casualties over the course of the war in Afghanistan. It is estimated that one person in every six has some form of disability. The national mine survey covering 979 villages of Afghanistan's 19,924 villages found 20,316 deaths and 15,985 injuries from landmines between 1979 and 1993.[31] It is currently estimated that 20 to 25 people fall victim to landmines every day, and that of the 8000 people those numbers represent annually, 50 percent die.

The VVAF field survey supports those estimates. Of the families interviewed, 13.6 percent had a family member involved in a mine accident--and 59 percent of the accidents were fatal. Forty-eight percent of accidents resulted in amputation and another 13 percent in blindness. Eighty-two percent of landmine casualties involve civilians and the overwhelming number of accidents involve adult males. But landmines also pose significant risk to children in the country. At least 20 percent of mine victims are children under 15. Accidents to boys accounted for eighty-three percent of child mine accidents and 44 percent of mine accidents to boys were fatal. The fatality rate for girls was the same. Women represented the remaining ten percent of mine victims.

The field survey demonstrates the significant financial impact of landmine accidents on mine victims and their families. Victims' families spent a total of $197,880 on accident-related expenditures. The average expenditure per family was $338. Eighty-seven percent of the families of survivors went into debt because of the accident. Fifty-six percent had to sell assets to pay for medicines, transportation, treatment costs, food during treatment, and blood. The impact transcends the time of treatment. Unemployment for adult males rose from six percent to 54 percent as a result of a landmine incident.

Rehabilitative care has not been able to meet the needs of those injured by landmines. At various times, facilities have had to close or relocate because of the continuing conflict. UNICEF has found some reluctance on the part of Afghan refugee parents to have their disabled children take part in physiotherapy and educational programs. Only one-third of those recommended for physiotherapy actually received the service.[32]

One of every three Afghans was displaced over the course of the war. At the height of the war, one of every two refugees in the world came from Afghanistan and at one point, Pakistan held the largest concentration of the world's refugees. Landmines have inhibited the return of hundreds of thousands of these refugees. While 1.6 million refugees have returned to Afghanistan from Pakistan, another 1.4 million have not. One million refugees have also returned to Afghanistan from Iran, but another 1.6 million have stayed behind. Eighteen percent of refugee families interviewed in Pakistan by VVAF said they had left Afghanistan because of landmines. Thirty-one percent said that mines had prevented their growing crops and 38 percent had lost at least one animal to landmines. Twenty-one percent reported that one or more members of their family had been involved in a mine incident.

When refugees have returned to the country, the incidents of mine accidents have increased dramatically. During the mass return in 1992, casualty rates jumped to two to three times the rate recorded during the same period in the previous year. One study carried out during a six month period in Peshawar in 1992 indicated that 77 percent of mine victims were returnees. Herat province has the second highest rate of mine casualties in the country and 90 percent of the refugees in Iran are expected to return to Herat. Repatriated and displaced families surveyed for this report in Herat were more than twice as likely to have suffered a mine accident than those who had stayed in Afghanistan. Returnee and displaced families were also about 20 percent less likely to own animals and 40 percent less likely to be farming than the families who had never left the country.

Displacement in some parts of Afghanistan continues, with significant exodus from Kabul. The majority of the displaced have gone to Jalalabad, where the first two camps were established for IDPs early 1993 (by early 1995, there were five such camps). IDPs in Jalalabad have fallen victim to landmines with UNOCHA reporting a significant increase in casualties after the influx of displaced from Kabul. Incidents were two and one half times higher in February 1994 than the average of 25 a month in the second half of 1993.[33] Most mine incidents have occurred when victims have left the camps to collected firewood or scrap metal, often disregarding boundaries established by deminers and previous mine awareness training.

Support for refugees has required significant resources from the international community. In the six months between October 1992 and March 1993, the cost of direct assistance to refugees in Pakistan was $8 million; the total appeal for emergency humanitarian assistance for Afghanistan was $97.3 million. UNHCR and the WFP have announced that they will end most assistance to Afghan refugees in Pakistan by September 1995. This will almost certainly precipitate a significant movement of refugees back to Afghanistan, and spark a consequent rise in the number of landmine fatalities.

Angola

The use of landmines in Angola began with the war against colonial Portugal, which erupted in January 1961. The fifteen year war finally resulted Angolan independence on 11 November 1975. Almost immediately, the forces which had fought the Portuguese--and each other--began one of the longest running civil wars in Africa. External support for the new government (formed by the Movemento por Popular Libertacao de Angola (MPLA)) came primarily from the Soviet Union and Cuba, while support for the Uniao Nacional para Independencia Total (UNITA) opposition came from South Africa and the United States. After years of fighting, UN-brokered negotiations resulted in the 31 May 1991 signing of the *Bicesse Accords* which called for national elections in September 1992. UNITA refused to accept the election results and returned to the battlefield in October 1992. The subsequent two years of particularly intense fighting brought greater destruction to the country than the previous 18 years of war.[34] Upwards of 500,000 people were killed; 150,000 died after the resumption of fighting in 1992.[35] Renewed negotiations resulted in the signing of a new peace agreement--the *Lusaka Accord*--in November 1994 and the deployment of UN peacekeeping forces.

While Portuguese, Cuban and South African forces used landmines in Angola, the overwhelming responsibility for their dissemination lies with UNITA and the Angolan army. The problem of landmines is particularly severe because almost no part of the country was untouched by the war. UNITA, from its base area in the southeast, sought to destabilize the government by making normal life as difficult as possible in as much of the country as it could. Widespread use of landmines was a critical part of the strategy and the mining of roads, paths and bridges was an important tactic. Government forces used mines to defend key economic installations and strategic sites: major roads, railroads, dams, oil installations, diamond mines and water pipelines were mined. Government-controlled population centers were also ringed with minefields. In addition to defending economic installations and important military bases with mines, the Angolan army laid mines to try to prevent UNITA forces from operating in the country.

16

The three decades of war have caused widespread social and economic disruption, leaving the infrastructure and economy of Angola ruined. Much of the renewed fighting in 1992 was concentrated around government-controlled provincial capitals or major towns, besieged by UNITA forces, which were all heavily mined. In parts of the country, fleeing soldiers on both sides mined hospitals, schools and markets.[36] Populations displaced by the fighting took refuge in the besieged towns. Unable to produce their own food, people have relied heavily on humanitarian relief efforts, which have been severely hampered by the mined infrastructure.[37]

Most of Angola's roads are known or suspected to be mined, making access to areas of the countryside outside the provincial capitals almost impossible. Supplies, equipment and personnel have been flown daily into these towns--a difficult operation due to the mining of airports.[38] Because of the inaccessibility of towns, the Angola relief operation has been one of the most complicated and expensive in the world. In 1994, over 200,000 tons of food were brought in to feed approximately two million people at a cost of $100 million.[39] In 1994, the Japanese government committed $2,435,000 for the World Food Program to demine and rehabilitate two major road corridors to facilitate the provision of humanitarian relief. In August 1994, however, a technical appraisal mission assessed the project's feasibility and concluded that the work should be carried out "in a post peace-agreement scenario."[40]

At certain points during the fighting, relief flights were suspended. This resulted in increased incidents of mine casualties as people were forced to search for food in heavily mined areas.[41] A survey carried out in one of the besieged towns found that the principal reason that people were being injured by landmines was their search for food.[42] Between February and September 1994, the population affected by the war increased by ten percent to 3.6 million; social services were near collapse and the inflation rate continued escalating.[43] The humanitarian crisis was exacerbated by a 70 percent loss of the maize harvest in the central *planalto* region due to drought.[44] Additionally, livestock grazing has been severely limited by landmines and the national herd has continued to be reduced in number.[45]

The suffering of Angola will not end with the possible coming of peace. Economic recovery will be hindered by landmines strewn along the country's 8577 km of paved roads and 3189 km of railroads. Mine clearance operations in Angola will be particularly difficult because of the extensive use of anti-handling and booby trap devices by UNITA.[46] Even as the cessation of fighting holds and displaced populations begin returning to their homes, food aid requirements will continue to be significant. Recently displaced populations and returnees are targeted for food relief in 1995, along with acutely affected populations in food deficit areas and besieged and cut-off towns. The 1995 UN Consolidated Appeal includes a figure of $37,490,755 for WFP food aid for Angola. The ability of these populations to become self sufficient will be affected in the longer term by the landmines sown through much of the country.

The United Nations estimates that there are between nine and 15 million landmines in Angola.[47] A 1995 UN appeal for Angola outlines priority mine action projects to "address access to 70% of the countryside."[48] It estimates that eight million Angolans, of a total population of 12.8 million, live in mine-infested areas of the country. Over two million of these people are in the former besieged cities and front line villages found primarily in the provinces of Huambo, Benguela, Bie and Uige.[49]

The demining capacity in Angola is severely limited and will remain so until effective cessation of fighting is ensured. Some mine clearance was begun by government and UNITA forces after the *Bicesse Accord* during the brief period of peace between May 1991 and the resumption of fighting in late 1992. Additionally, a German NGO, Cap Anamur, has been operating in the Cumene Province near Xangongo since the beginning of 1993. According to government sources, the joint Cap Anamur/Government of Angola operation has cleared and destroyed more than 50,000 antitank mines, 25,000 antipersonnel mines, 50,000 bombs, rockets and grenades, and more than 200 metric tons of small munitions, explosives and fuses.[50]

In March 1994, the Central Mines Action Office (CMAO) was established with Canadian funding of $277,000[51] as part of the United Nations' Humanitarian Assistance Coordination Unit (UCAH). CMAO began to gather mine-related data, to lay the groundwork for a national mine survey, and to work with the UN Angola Verification Mission (UNAVEM) to prepare a program for the mine clearance required for the UNAVEM III peacekeeping operation. Mine clearance during UNAVEM III operations will concentrate on roads, ports, bridges and other areas critical to the successful completion of its mission. Other priorities include mine awareness programs, a national mine survey, and the establishment of regional schools to train deminers. Plans call for training 1000 deminers in the first 18 months and by the end of the first two and a half years, a total of 3000.[52] Before the end of the UNAVEM III mission, program responsibility is to be shifted to UNDP and management to be carried out increasingly by Angolans. As quickly as possible, the program is to be transferred to the government. Bilateral donations are to replace UNAVEM funding for mine clearance in Angola.

A number of international aid and non-governmental organizations from a variety of countries have begun mine clearance and awareness operations in Angola. The overall UN mine clearance plan for Angola calls for the integration of the UN and NGO mine awareness projects into a coordinated national program. UNICEF has developed a proposal for mine awareness in all 18 provinces at a projected cost of $1.5 million. Children will be a particular target of the program that will include radio and media campaigns, distribution of posters and signposts, orientation of agricultural workers as the program's vanguard through the household security program, sensitization of opinion leaders to reach the wider community, and the involvement of demobilized soldiers and amputees in building awareness. The program will also encourage school involvement in mine awareness education.[53]

Exact numbers of mine casualties in Angola are impossible to obtain. Assessments of the problem are particularly difficult to make because of the extent of isolation of large parts of the country, which is due at least in part to the presence of landmines. Current estimates of amputees range from 40,000 to 70,000, with an additional 70,000 killed by landmines. According to the Viana Rehabilitation Center (VRC) in Luanda, there are 45,000 war-disabled persons in the country, of which 56 percent are missing a lower limb. This estimate probably does not include those disabled living in areas outside of government control.[54] In its recent assessment for a proposal for a mine awareness program for Angola, UNICEF put the number of amputees at over 70,000. Of that number it estimated that 8000 were children.[55] The direct cost for medical and rehabilitative care for 80,000 mine victims is estimated at $240 million.

In 1994, U.S. AID estimated the number of new mine injuries occurring in Angola at "likely not less than 150-200 per week."[56] Mine casualty rates are expected to increase as the cessation of fighting holds and the movement of displaced populations begins. Other pressures have already contributed to fluctuations of casualty rates observed at hospitals and rehabilitation centers. Food pressures in besieged cities and towns have resulted in increased civilian mine injuries. Reliable information regarding victim profiles is still limited. However, data gathered by the ICRC in 1990 and Africa Watch in 1992 provide useful information about people affected by landmines in Angola.[57] Approximately one-half of the victims admitted to ICRC's center for amputees in Bomba Alto near Huambo in 1990 were soldiers and the other half were civilians. Both ICRC and Africa Watch data show most casualties to be adult men. UNICEF has estimated that 11.4 percent of the amputees in Angola are children. Africa Watch's survey was consistent with this estimate as was the number of child patients at the ICRC facility.[58]

Angola's prosthetic and rehabilitation capabilities fall far short of demand. It is estimated that less than ten percent of amputees have prosthetic devices.[59] Until the forced abandonment of their facilities, the ICRC had produced more than 12,000 prostheses since beginning operations in Angola in 1980.[60] Swedish and Dutch Red Cross supported facilities at Neves Bendinha and Viana, respectively, were operating at 50 percent capacity, producing 1,000 prostheses annually. In 1995, the World Health Organization (WHO) appealed for $1,118,300 for programs to support demining personnel and civilian mine casualties. WHO plans to train paramedics for each demining site, to make available an operational blood transfusion unit for testing, banking and transfusion, and to support prosthetics rehabilitation centers in Luanda and Benguela.[61] Even with the reopening of facilities and possible new programs with the cessation of fighting, supply will not begin to meet the demand for prostheses in Angola in the near future.

With the renewed prospects for peace in late 1994, UNHCR began updating repatriation plans for 280,000 refugees from Zaire, Zambia and other countries; 100,000 are expected to return in 1995. Because of the extent of the landmine problem, UNHCR has requested that certain sites "which are of particular importance to the repatriation operation...be given due consideration in the demining strategy."[62] These include ten entry points and transit centers in the provinces of Cabinda, Zaire, Uige, and Moxico. The agency also noted that surveys of routes in Uige and Zaire had been conducted in 1994 and found them to be mine free, with the caveat that fighting had occurred in the area in November 1994 which might have affected that status.

The 1995 UN Mine Action Budget for Angola includes an appeal for $300,000 to clear assembly areas for IDPs and returning refugees. The mine action plan recognizes that clearing assembly areas "is intended to provide a verification and spot demining capability to render these assembly areas and the surrounding access routes mine-safe. This project represents the essential and immediate initial requirements for relocation, following which there will have to be a detailed demining of the prime agricultural lands surrounding villages to which these displaced Angolans will be returning..."[63]

Cambodia

There have been more than two decades of war in Cambodia, beginning with a 1970 coup that deposed then-Prince Norodom Sihanouk, massive bombing by the United States during the Vietnam War, the devastating years of Khmer Rouge rule, and the invasion and ten-year occupation of the country by Vietnam. A UN-brokered peace agreement in 1993 resulted in nationwide elections followed by the formation of a new coalition government. But the October 1991 *Agreements on a Comprehensive Political Settlement of the Cambodia Conflict* have not brought true peace to the country. The Khmer Rouge broke the agreement, refused to participate in the elections, and continue to wage war against the government.

Landmines were first used in Cambodia during the Vietnam War. However, the majority of mines were laid between 1979 and 1991, increasing dramatically with the Vietnamese invasion. The fighting in Cambodia has been fluid, with shifting battlegrounds and front lines. Minefield has been sown on top of minefield, as territory has been repeatedly won and lost. All forces have used mines both to defend their own forces and strategic positions and as offensive weapons to demoralize and impoverish communities. An estimated eight million landmines contaminate the country. Both government forces and the KR continue to use landmines in their ongoing conflict.

By June 1995, the Cambodia Mine Action Center (CMAC) had verified 1982 minefields in 15 provinces and the autonomous city of Sihanoukville. Many more are likely to be added to the list as assessments continue. Much of the work identifying minefields has been limited by inaccessibility and security problems. While mines are found in areas that have been affected by the conflict throughout about 50 percent of the country, covering about 3200 sq. km of Cambodia, most landmines are concentrated in the northern, eastern and western parts of the country.

Eighty-five percent of Cambodia's population makes its living from agriculture. Over the course of the war, the amount of land under cultivation in Cambodia has fallen between 600,000-900,000 hectares. Of that amount, an estimated 200,000 hectares are mine-affected. Two hectares is considered the minimum necessary for a family to produce sufficient paddy rice to meet its basic needs, but many Cambodians cultivate less than that amount because of landmines; many Cambodians cultivate no land at all. The 200,000 mine-contaminated hectares represent a loss of the means of self-sufficiency for approximately 100,000 families. The average annual rice production per hectare is 1.2 tons per hectare, among the lowest in the world;[64] 240,000 tons of rice are lost to production because of mine-contaminated land. In effect, landmines are a direct contributor to food loss, and the resulting malnutrition, in Cambodia.

The field survey for this report interviewed 33,961 individuals in six provinces in the country.[65] Fifty-nine percent of the 6090 households surveyed reported that they could cultivate more land if not for the presence of landmines. The total additional land that would be cultivated was equal to 135 percent of that currently under cultivation. Seventy percent of those surveyed were cultivating at the time of the survey; the average amount of land cultivated was .8 hectares per household. In Battambang and Banteay Meanchey, two of the most mine-contaminated provinces in the country, up to 50 percent of those surveyed were discouraged from farming because of landmines. Additionally, 68 percent reported that they had changed other work patterns or, in some cases, had stopped certain activities altogether because of landmines. Activities affected included field work, cutting wood, and to a lesser extent, fishing, cutting thatch or tending animals. Additionally, 13 percent of families surveyed had lost an average of 2.5 animals per household to landmines.

Agricultural production in Cambodia depends on rainfall and a network of irrigation canals throughout the country. In sections of the country that have been heavily mined, water sources, including canals, have been mined. In Banan district of Battambang province, water gates and canal banks of one commune's irrigation system were so heavily mined that the system was too dangerous to repair and the commune lost the use of half of the land that it had cultivated previously. Forests in the western and southeastern sections of Cambodia are contaminated with landmines, as reflected by the fact that the majority of recorded mine incidents in Cambodia occur in wooded areas.

The road system of Cambodia has sustained significant damage during the years of fighting and is estimated to be operating at 40 to 50 percent of capacity. The World Bank found that the widespread presence of mines, particularly on the secondary and tertiary roads, posed serious problems and aggravated the precarious economic situation of some provinces in the country.[66] Primary roads are now generally free of mines. But many secondary and tertiary roads remain mined, as do those leading into and out of KR contested territory. Most bridges in the country were destroyed at least once during the conflict and the transportation system remains under attack in areas of conflict. Many portions of the national rail system remain either mined or under attack.[67] As of June 1995, CMAC was unable to give an overview of the extent of mining of either the road or irrigation systems of the country, or how much had been demined.[68]

Despite the recognition that humanitarian mine clearance is pivotal to Cambodia's future development, the planning for that clearance has at times lacked clarity. The initial plan of the UN mission to Cambodia (UNTAC) did not include the training of Cambodian deminers for an indigenous mine clearance program. When the mission plan was expanded in January 1992 to include the training of 7000 indigenous deminers, there remained a significant gap: there was no plan for putting trained deminers to work clearing landmines. (This was almost two years after the UN demining program in Afghanistan went through the same process and recognized the need for an organized plan for demining operations to incorporate newly trained deminers.)

The demining that initially took place was carried out to ensure successful completion of UNTAC's mission. It was in mid-August 1992 that the first operation paid for by the UN took place after an elaborate plan was worked out so that an NGO would assume liability risk rather than the United Nations. The idea of establishing a Cambodian entity to oversee the long-term mine clearance of the country emerged during the UNTAC period. The Cambodia Mine Action Center (CMAC) was established in July 1993 as the UNTAC mission was beginning to end. The United Nations wanted to withdraw from the country having completed a successful mission. But without a mechanism to ensure UN support for demining, donor countries would not commit significant financial resources or military assets so CMAC could continue its work. As a result, CMAC was on the verge of collapse when UNTAC personnel were withdrawn in November of 1993. As foreign military demining supervisors and trainers were withdrawn with no commitment for replacements in sight, the UN quickly came to understand the seriousness of the problem and ultimately worked out a mechanism for UN oversight of CMAC during the two-year transition to full Cambodianization.

In 1993 CMAC projected that it might take 250 years to demine Cambodia. After looking more closely at priority areas, CMAC reported that the main problems stemming from landmines could be controlled in five to eight years; demining could continue at a reduced scale, it reported, for another 20 years under Cambodian funding and leadership. Priority is given to demining land for resettlement and cultivation. Demining for development, such as road clearance and infrastructure repair or expansion, is considered low priority unless special funding increases CMAC's capacity. CMAC reports that demining accomplished through 1994 allowed the resettlement of over 13,000 IDPs or the equivalent land for production of 650 tons of rice. CMAC's activity report for the period from March 1992 to May 1995 shows that 233 minefields (including 52 during the UNTAC period) were cleared in eight provinces. During clearance operations, 61,352 antipersonnel mines, 435 antitank mines and 423,708 UXOs were found. The two-year budget for CMAC in 1994/95 was $20 million.

Cambodia is one of the most mine-disabled countries in the world. The most common figure for the number of amputee landmine victims is 35,000. Current estimates of casualties are 100-200 a month. Village-level research for this report and data shows that these estimates are low. The number of casualties per month can shift dramatically, as they did during a military offensive in the first months of 1995. The health care costs associated with landmine casualties are far greater than the Cambodian medical system can handle. Less than 53 percent of the population has access to health services and the Cambodian government allocates about $.20 per capita per year for health services.[69] Most surgical facilities are overcrowded, unsanitary and long distances from the majority of mine victims' homes.

Seven percent of households surveyed for this report had one or more family members involved in a mine incident. It has previously been held that for every mine victim in Cambodia who survives an landmine incident, another one to two do not live after a mine blast. In the population surveyed for this report, 306 of a total of 445 mine victims had survived the incident--a survival rate of 69 percent. The mortality rate did not differ significantly between sexes. Landmines predominantly affect adult males in Cambodia. In the VVAF survey, 86.5 percent of mine victims were adult males, seven percent of victims were under 15 years of age and six percent were women. Sixty-four percent were civilians and 36 percent of the injured were soldiers. Seventy-seven military landmine casualties interviewed for this report in early 1995 at Phnom Penh and Battambang military hospitals, 43 percent were between ten and 16 years of age.

Eighty-four percent of survivors surveyed reported having had surgery from one to 15 times as a result of the mine accident. Thirty percent had more than one operation. Fifty percent of the landmine incidents resulted in some form of amputation and 26 percent involved multiple injuries. Three-quarters of the families of survivors had to spend money for expenses related to the mine accident. Overall, more than $41,800 was spent taking care of victims--an average of $138 per victim. This is almost the equivalent of the total annual income for a family in rural Cambodia. Sixty-one percent of families of survivors of mine blasts went into debt because of the accident.

The United Nations has estimated that the average lifetime cost for medical and rehabilitative care for mine victims is $3000 per victim. Assuming an amputee population of 35,000, the health care burden is $105 million in Cambodia alone. Using a conservative number of 100 additional survivors per month, this would add an additional annual burden of $3.6 million. The production of prostheses in Cambodia has grown significantly since the early 1990s. By 1993, the rate of production of prosthetic devices in Cambodia was 6000 limbs annually. While limbs have become increasingly available, access and follow-up remain problems, especially among children--who need prosthetic refitting as they grow. Adults need new limbs every three to five years. For many rural amputees, loss of earnings as a result of time away from the village in order to get a limb and the affect on the family economy must be balanced against perceived advantages of receiving a limb.

Prosthetic devices alone do not necessarily resolve problems faced by amputees in Cambodia. Vocational rehabilitation is extremely limited. But skills training, without employment opportunities, is done in vain. The need for training and reintegration into the community is apparent: unemployment among adult males interviewed increased from 13 percent before the accident to 40 percent after; for females it increased from 12 percent to 29 percent.

The presence of landmines has had a significant impact on the Cambodian refugee population. While all refugees were repatriated in time to participate in the UN-supervised election (and no landmine casualties were registered during their return), the real impact of landmines was on the repatriation plan itself, and on the lives of the returnees once they were resettled. The plan originally called for 85,000 Cambodian refugee families to receive the two hectares of land per family considered necessary for self-sufficiency. This represented a total of about 170,000 hectares of land, 128,000 of which was to be in Pursat, Battambang, Banteay Meanchey and Siem Reap provinces where most refugees wanted to resettle. But landmine contamination in the provinces of choice was so severe that ultimately (of the 362,000 who repatriated with UNHCR) only 2435 families--10,261 people--received land under the original plan. Instead of receiving land, over 85 percent of the returnees received reintegration money and food for 400 days.

Landmines have also affected Cambodia's internally displaced population. It was thought that much of the IDP population--which reached 186,000 prior to the peace accords--would be able to resettle before repatriation of refugees began. But the incidence of mines in their home villages proved to be greater than estimated, forestalling their return and making continued assistance to them necessary. Over one-half of the IDP places of origin were mined. Some IDPs have had access to agricultural land, but a much larger group is without access to land, subsisting on logging or collecting firewood in forested areas--which are also mined.

Croatia and Bosnia-Herzegovina

Croatia and Bosnia-Herzegovina have been the site of intense conflict since mid-1991, when the Yugoslav federation began to disintegrate. The past four years of war have ravaged disputed areas, killed and wounded hundreds of thousands of civilians, and displaced more than three million people. Landmines are being used by all sides in the conflict and nearly all of them are of domestic origin. The growth of military industries, including the production of landmines, had been encouraged under the presidency of Josep Broz Tito, particularly in Bosnia-Herzegovina. Personnel of the United Nations Protection Force (UNPROFOR) report that mines are still being manufactured. The continuing fighting in Bosnia-Herzegovina and Croatia has made many government and military officials hesitant to provide information regarding the location of mines and their impact. Until the conflict has ended, the full extent of landmine damage will be impossible to assess.

Some minefield maps and records exist, more often in Croatia than in Bosnia. However, UNPRO-FOR officials consider them unreliable due to the shifting nature of the conflict. Many areas have been mined and remined by opposing factions in their attempts to strengthen control over contested territory or disrupt supply efforts. Mines have mostly been hand-laid, sometimes in patterns to deliberately hamper detection. A number of non-traditional mine techniques have been identified as in use in the former Yugoslavia. For example, trip wire mines have been used on roads to attack vehicles in sensitive areas. Minimum-metal mines have been stacked three high, the top two with their fuzes removed to avoid detection. Forests are reported to have been heavily mined with antipersonnel mines to prevent infiltration. As in the other countries researched for this report, there have been few traditional "tactical" minefields laid, due to the irregular nature of the conflict.

While some areas of Croatia and Bosnia-Herzegovina are badly affected by mines, these areas seem to be limited to those directly involved in the fighting. Mines are found in the UN Protected Areas (UNPAs) along the borders between Croatia, Bosnia-Herzegovina and Serbia-Montenegro, in the conflict areas in Dalmatia, and in vast sections of Central Bosnia. The Croatian Ministry of Reconstruction has reported that landmines affect towns, villages, tourist centers, industrial plants, energy supply facilities, streets, paths, railroads, waterways, forests and national parks, and the 1000 km border area between Croatia and Bosnia-Herzegovina. Mines have also been laid along the Croatian border with Hungary.

Mines have been deployed extensively in frontline areas. In Croatia, these have included the cities of Vukovar, Dubrovnik, Split, Zadar, and Osijek and the Krajina area (including Knin). In Bosnia, mines have been used in Banja Luka, Bugojno, Travnik, Visoko Malglaj, Tesanj, Zepce, Gorazde, Gornji Vakuf, Kladanj, Vitez, Mostar, Srebrenica, Tuzla, Medugorje and Bihac. Many of these areas have been very heavily affected. Mines have also been employed by all sides to the conflict in Sarajevo, Bosnia's capital. In Bosnia-Herzegovina, landmines were widely used during the Serb campaigns of "ethnic cleansing" (using terror tactics to empty towns of non-Serbs) in the Drina River valley (eastern Bosnia-Herzegovina) and towns around Banja Luka (northwest Bosnia). Around the town of Brcko, the Serbs established a corridor leading from Serbia to Serbian-controlled regions in Bosnia and Croatia. The corridor is heavily mined. The conflict over control of land and an existing railroad route across that part of the Bihac pocket that links Serb holdings in Croatia with Serb lands in Bosnia, and Serbia proper to the east, has also involved the use of mines.

Prior to the war, Croatia was self-sufficient in food production. According to the Croatian Ministry of Reconstruction, however, the country's agricultural sector has incurred an annual net loss of $230 million because of land removed from production due to landmines. Croatia's logging and tourism industries have incurred annual losses estimated at $70 million due to the presence of landmines.[70] In Bosnia-Herzegovina, no government estimate of lost production has been made. In central Bosnia, where the majority of landmines are believed to have been laid, some of the most productive soil in the country is sown with mines.

Field surveys undertaken for this report provide clear indicators on the extent of landmine-related problems in Bosnia. Information on the impact of mines was obtained through interviews with 14,090 households in four survey cycles conducted in 73 sites in central and eastern Bosnia between May 1994 and April 1995.[71] Landmines were reported by the households interviewed to inhibit agricultural production in 17 out of the first 41 sites surveyed. Households reported that access to land would have been 20 to 50 percent greater if not for the presence of landmines. At one site, forest production was also affected. In the Zenica area, 550 households were cultivating various crops. Overall, the economic effect of the presence of landmines on those farmers is estimated to amount to approximately $640,000 per agricultural season.[72] In the Mostar area, large stretches of abandoned land in the Doljani and Bjelo Polji valleys are not being cultivated because of mines. According to UNPROFOR assessments, millions of landmines have been laid in Croatia and Bosnia-Herzegovina since 1992. An estimated 1.5 million landmines are believed to have been planted in Bosnia-Herzegovina, and the numbers are increasing. One-third of Croatia, especially the Krajina region, is affected by one to three million mines.

Hydroelectric installations and transmission lines in Bosnia-Herzegovina have been severely affected by landmines. In the southern region of Bosnia-Herzegovina, minefields have halted a $926,586 project to rehabilitate the electrical grid in Medugorje. Another $142,552 power-line project underway in a mined area of the Doljani Valley near Jablanica was put out of service by landmines until an additional $64,148 was spent to install a new power line to complete the project. Croatian military officials claimed that demining the area would be difficult because they lost their information about the location of the mines. Landmines are also preventing a $712,758 rehabilitation project of the electrical power grid from D. Grabonica to Dreznica. At the Ricci junction (also known as Tomanovic), reconstruction cannot continue because of mines. No projection has been made on what it will cost to rehabilitate the line in the direction of Vrdl. To repair the line to Jasenjani will cost an estimated $33,500.

Due to the continuing conflict, no widespread mine clearance has been undertaken in either Croatia or Bosnia-Herzegovina. Under existing agreements, the UNPROFOR Force Engineers are only authorized to clear roads and other mined areas that need to be breached for UN or NGO purposes;

all other clearance is to be undertaken by the warring factions, with UNPROFOR supervision. From March through September 1992, UNPROFOR-led mine clearance teams identified and cleared 400 minefields in Sector West, one of the four UN Protected Areas in Croatia (which was recently recaptured by the Croatian government). Mines discovered during clearance operations have frequently been lifted for use elsewhere, as it is said to be beyond UNPROFOR's mandate to insist that mines be destroyed where found.

In 1992, the Croatian government estimated that $198 million would be needed over four years for priority demining in Croatia. In late 1993, it reported that approximately 35,000 mines had been removed from areas no longer in dispute. Total landmine clearance costs are projected to amount to $400 million over nine years. No similar projections have yet been made for Bosnia-Herzegovina.

Mine awareness programs have been initiated by UNICEF and the Croatian Red Cross in Croatia and by UNICEF, the International Rescue Committee, and Save the Children (US), in Bosnia-Herzegovina. UNICEF programs have involved school activities, teacher training, and the production of videos and other materials on mine awareness. There is concern that government officials, humanitarian agencies, and UNPROFOR have not had an overall strategy incorporating mine clearance with mine awareness and victim assistance. UNICEF sponsored a meeting on mine education in Mostar, bringing together local leaders, NGOs, and UN agencies, which noted a need for common symbols for marking mined areas and for a focal point in the government for data collection on mine victims and incidents. In Croatia, UNICEF also held a national symposium on landmines, which resulted in a National Plan of Action on landmines in Croatia.

Because of the war and the continued use of landmines, information about landmine victims is seen as having strategic value. This view means that, in some cases, physicians, hospital staff, humanitarian aid workers, heads of households and key informants refused to participate in landmine-related research. Additionally, inconsistent or non-existent record-keeping systems in some hospitals and clinics make reliable determination of numbers and profiles of mine victims impossible. Lack of coordination among many NGOs and UN agencies involved in landmine-related problems has resulted in duplication of records and statistics on mine victims, who may be treated by several different rehabilitation agencies and registered with each one.

As of March 1, 1995, the Center for the Development of Disaster Management Systems (CDDMS) of the School of Medicine at the University of Zagreb reported that of 8449 persons were injured by in Croatia since the start of the war; 643 had been involved in landmine incidents. CDDMS reported that 31.2 percent of amputations in Croatia were landmine-related. Figures available through Handicap International workshops in the Zenica and Tuzla regions of Bosnia-Herzegovina show that landmines are even more frequently the cause of amputations in those regions of the country: landmines were cited as the cause of injury among 45 percent of amputees treated in Zenica and 55 percent of amputees treated in Tuzla.

The World Health Organization (WHO) supplies prostheses in Croatia and the United Nations Protected Areas and directly supervises the fitting of prosthetic devices in two orthopedic hospitals in Zagreb and in Split. In 1994, 42 percent of the 230 patients treated at the Zagreb facility were mine victims: only one was a woman. There were no victims under 15 years of age. During the same period, the Split hospital served 102 patients, of which 45 percent were victims of mine incidents. Two of them were women and none were under 15 years of age. UNICEF reported that between March 1993 and March 1994, 76 children died and 130 were wounded by mines in Croatia.

In Bosnia, landmine disabled people were identified in all nine regions included in a field survey for this report. Only five of 41 communities surveyed did not report any landmine incidents. The highest prevalence of incidents was in Gornji Bakuf, Vares, and Zenica (Bosnia-Herzegovina), where more than 12 percent of households were affected. There was roughly the same risk for Muslim and Bosnian Serb households, but more than double the risk in ethnic Croat households. Urban sites were no less likely to be mined than rural sites. Households in sites which had been believed safe (according to UNHCR) were no less at risk of being mined than sites located in zones near the front line. In households surveyed in central Bosnia, more than four-fifths of those interviewed did not know whether there were landmines near their homes. However, one out of three had received some information about landmines. Among those who had received mine awareness information, most said they had received their information from the local army or local authorities. Others had received information on landmines from the media, and to a lesser extent from friends and relatives or from the local Red Cross. One in four householders were refugees.

By mid-1994, landmines were responsible for the majority of UNPROFOR casualties in Croatia and Bosnia-Herzegovina. From April 1992 through April 1995, despite mine awareness training provided to UNPROFOR personnel, a total of 166 mine incidents were reported, resulting in nineteen deaths and 190 injuries. Antipersonnel mines were the cause of 102 of these incidents, 51 of which occurred in Bosnia-Herzegovina, and the other 51 in the UNPAs in Croatia.

The conditions for rehabilitation of landmine victims in Croatia are reportedly much better than in Bosnia-Herzegovina: there are more treatment facilities, including 12 private workshops producing prosthetic devices, and there are subsidies available for victims of the war. Nonetheless, only 60 percent of those needing prostheses in Croatia have received them and the situation in Bosnia-Herzegovina is much worse.

In central Bosnia, Handicap International and Voluntary Relief Doctors (VRD) train local prosthetic technicians and produce prostheses. The World Health Organization is also in the process of establishing a clinic in Mostar which is projected to begin operations in the fall of 1995. From February 1993 through October 1994, Handicap International's prostheses workshops in Tuzla and Zenica provided 1057 lower-limb amputees with prostheses; 740 amputees were on their waiting list for prostheses. VRD, which operates a rehabilitation center in central Bosnia serving Zenica and surrounding towns, reported a waiting list of 1400 patients. (Of the 711 amputees it treated from June 1994 to March 1995, 62.6 percent were landmine victims.)

The World Health Organization in Croatia estimates the material costs of a temporary below-knee prosthesis with a fixed ankle at $143 and a temporary above-knee prosthesis up to $428. The production of more permanent below-knee prostheses costs $1069 per device and $3564 per above-knee prostheses using the most economical knee available--which costs $2138. Considering only the needs of patients in rehabilitation with VRD, there would need to be a minimum production of 1000 prostheses, with a minimum material cost of $1,496,793. Assuming actual production capacity of 28 prosthetic devices per month and treatment for 350 amputees per year, and a constant percentage of patients under 15 years of age and between ages 16 to 20, the VRD rehabilitation center would require $2,138,275 in material costs for one cycle of four years. Considering that the majority of victims are between the ages of twenty and forty years of age, with an average disabled life of 35 years (during which time they will need at least eight prosthetic refittings), it has been estimated that each victim will need $9622 in actual material costs for rehabilitation during that period. The rehabilitation of all cases reported registered in the former Yugoslavia was estimated at $27,227,370.

The Croatian Government Office for Displaced Persons and Refugees (ODPR), reported in April 1995 that there were 192,163 Croatians displaced from the approximately one-third of Croatia occupied by rebel Serbs, and an additional 185,134 Croat or Muslim refugees in Croatia who fled Bosnia-Herzegovina and other republics of the former Yugoslavia. 3662 individuals were classified as "returnees" to their home villages in Croatia. Previously, the Croatian Red Cross reported that 150,000 refugees and IDPs had been able to return to areas in Croatia where the conflict has been reduced (Dubrovnic, Split, and Sibenik). An additional 97,000 refugees (mostly Serbian) were reportedly living within the UNPAs. In August 1995, the Croatian government retook the Krajina territory held by rebel Serbs resulting in tens of thousands of new refugees. Those who have lived in the disputed areas, and those who will attempt to settle there after the war, face landmines used in the conflict: along roads and mountain paths, in villages, schools, places of worship, forests, and waterways.

Within Bosnia-Herzegovina, UNHCR reported an estimated 1,327,000 displaced and 1,422,000 war-affected individuals in mid-1995. An upsurge in fighting in June, July and August created even higher numbers of refugees throughout Bosnia-Herzegovina. A field report issued by UNHCR Zenica stated: "Land mines continue to pose a serious threat in central Bosnia," not only for UNPROFOR and aid workers, but also the civilian population living in the midst of the conflict. Among refugee, displaced and war-affected populations, the largest percentage (nearly one-forth of the total) are from the central Bosnian region of Zenica, where 12 percent of households surveyed reported that they were involved in landmine incidents.

Mozambique

Until recently, Mozambique has been at war since the early 1960s, when the Front for the Liberation of Mozambique (Frelimo) began the fight for independence from Portugal. Within two years of independence in 1975, Rhodesia organized and armed the Mozambique National Resistance (Renamo) to fight against the newly-established Frelimo government. After Rhodesia's independence--when it became Zimbabwe--support for Renamo came from South Africa, which supported the Mozambican insurrection until at least late 1989. The conflict continued unabated until the October 1992 *Rome Peace Agreement* between the government and Renamo opposition forces.

Most of the forces fighting in the country over the past three decades actively engaged in mine warfare. However, the vast majority of mines were laid after independence in 1975, during the conflict between the government and Renamo. Rhodesian troops and South African forces planted mines in their campaign against the government in support of Renamo. Frelimo began to protect installations near the Rhodesian border and subsequently laid large minefields along the border with South Africa.[73] During the fighting between Renamo and the government, Mozambique's infrastructure, especially that related to health, transport and education, was a consistent target of attempts to destabilize and undermine the Frelimo government. Documents captured from a Renamo base detailed plans to destroy the transportation system and disrupt local economies.[74]

Both Renamo and the government used mines defensively around their military bases. In all provinces, former military camps, villages used as bases, and buildings such as schools or administrative centers used as headquarters, were surrounded by minefields. Mines were also laid around important economic infrastructure, by the government to protect the infrastructure and by Renamo to prevent reconstruction and repair. Airstrips were mined, especially in unstable or highly contested areas. Mines were laid along railway tracks and at river crossings to prevent enemy expansion. Bridges were destroyed and their pylons mined. Both sides mined roads in areas under their influence to prevent invasion.

In central Mozambique and in other areas, government troops and Renamo used mines offensively against civilian communities, denying access to fields, water sources and fishing points. In southern provinces, Renamo laid mines to discourage the return of displaced persons to their homes. In Inhambane and Gaza provinces, water wells, clinics, schools, small factories, cashew-nut groves and cattle-dip tanks were mined. Some cemeteries and access paths to them were mined, disrupting traditional religious practices. In addition, the threat of mines has been used as psychological warfare against civilians--in the Gorgongosa region civilians were told that areas were mined, when they were not.

Between February and June 1994, the first nationwide mine assessment identified 981 mined areas. The assessment found that although there are some large minefields in the country, there were frequently just a few mines are scattered over a vast area, effectively blocking its access and use. These findings have been confirmed by the first reports of demining teams in Mozambique. There are an estimated one million mines in Mozambique.[75] The most severely mined provinces in the country are Maputo, Inhambane, Sofala, Manica and Tete. Gaza is heavily mined and Zambezia is believed to be heavily mined. All borders are assumed to be mined.

Different regions of the country have had comparative advantage in growing certain foods, but landmines laid on many of the major roads of the country had disrupted trade and made exchange of food and other goods impossible. Disruption of transportation between the north and south of the country affected both family and large-scale farms, resulting in a sharp decline in nationally-produced foods. Food security is a continuing problem and the impact of landmines has made a bad situation worse. Landmines are one of the key factors contributing to chronic and acute malnutrition in Mozambique.

Sixty-three percent of Mozambique's road system is in such disrepair that traffic movement is difficult or impossible. Major roads were affected by landmines. By mid-1994 8000 km of roads were listed as known or suspected to be mined in the provinces of Manica, Sofala, Zambezia, Tete and Niassa--one-quarter of Mozambique's road system. There has also been extensive destruction of bridges and their supports, which are mined throughout the country. One-half of all district capitals were accessible only with difficulty. Mozambique's cities, particularly Maputo, provide the country with a very limited industrial base which is highly dependent on imported supplies, many of which were unavailable due to the risks and costs of transporting goods over mined roads. Additionally, the mining of the transportation system, as well as insecurity due to the fighting, had forced Zimbabwe, Zambia and other landlocked "frontline" states to reroute much of their road freight by way of South Africa--at an added annual cost of $300 million and a consequent loss of needed revenue to Mozambique.[76] While major roads are clear, paths and tracks are still mined.

The main power plant in the country and one of the most important in the entire region, the Cahora Bassa Dam in Tete province, has been significantly affected by landmines. Its power lines extend 980 km through Tete, Manica and Gaza provinces to South Africa. While the dam itself has remained in working condition, power distribution fell to less than one percent of capacity because of mined and destroyed transmission lines. This reduction in output has caused imports of electricity to increase from $1 million in 1980 to $10 million in 1988. The projected cost to repair the power lines is $125-150 million. This figure does not include the cost of demining paths leading to the lines. Other power generating facilities and power lines are also ringed by landmines in Maputo, Gaza and Nampula provinces, endangering populations in their vicinity. Clearance of this infrastructure is not included as a priority in the UN's Mine Clearance Plan for Mozambique.

After the signing of the peace accords, the United Nations outlined a framework for demining Mozambique. The plan focussed on a national mine survey, emergency clearance of roads to allow for repatriation and the provision of humanitarian aid to isolated areas, establishment of a training center to provide Mozambique with a long-term indigenous demining capacity, and mine awareness programs for the resident population and returning refugees. Despite this detailed plan, the demining program has been plagued by conflict and delay, both between the government and Renamo in reaching final approval of the plan, and within the United Nations bureaucracy. Clearance of high priority roads was to begin by August 1993, but did not start until almost one year later. (There was also a controversy about awarding of clearance contracts to a consortium that included companies involved in munitions production and export.) By the time that road clearance finally began many agencies felt that the mine situation had become clearer, and that other priorities should be addressed first. But the United Nations felt compelled to adhere to the original plan, fearing that any attempt to modify it would result in further delays.

During the delay period, a pilot project from January 1993 to March 1994 cleared 179 km of priority roads in Manica and Sofala provinces, finding only six landmines, mainly at the bases of bridges. But during clearance operations, almost 60,000 metal fragments had to be investigated and 11,454 UXOs disposed of. Finally in July 1994 demining work under the UN plan began in Sofala and

Manica provinces and by the end of the year, 1644.1 kilometers of road had been cleared. Nineteen antipersonnel mines and one antitank mine were found along with 204 UXOs and 14,500 pieces of small arms ammunition. In September, UNOMOZ began implementing an "accelerated mine clearance program" that placed 400 deminers in priority areas in Maputo province. By the end of the year it had cleared 38,340 sq meters of land, encountering 279 antipersonnel landmines.

The problems blocking the implementation of the demining plan resulted in delays in beginning mine clearance training. Plans had to be revised to provide for accelerated training of Mozambican deminers with the target of training and equipping 450 deminers by the end of the UNOMOZ mandate. The plan called for indigenous capacity building to create an administrative structure to run the long-term demining program in the country. Bids for proposals were called for in October 1994. The UN contracted with Defense Systems Ltd., a multi-national conglomerate, to establish and run the program and train 45 Mozambican personnel to run demining operations by the end of December 1995.

Original estimates projected that priority mine clearance in Mozambique would take between seven to ten years and cost $30-40 million. Although clearance to allow the rehabilitation of much of the infrastructure necessary for the reconstruction of the country was recognized to be of great importance, most of these projects have not been budgeted or financed under the UN program. Such clearance is said to fall under "development" rather than "emergency" requirements. Clearance of the major infrastructure and agricultural land in Mozambique's rural areas will take years. The mine clearance program has been funded in part by the UNOMOZ budget and by bilateral contributions. Budgeted needs of $14,329,901 for 1993 and $18,300,000 for 1994 were not met by donations, which totalled $23,840,790. Mine awareness was undertaken through UNHCR in cooperation with a number of NGOs, both in Mozambique and in neighboring countries with refugee populations. Mine awareness campaigns began in mid-1993. UNHCR's initial budget for the campaign was $2.1 million.

Only 30 per cent of Mozambicans live within what UNICEF describes as "a reasonable distance" from primary health facilities. Along with destruction of other infrastructure, Renamo destroyed 36 percent of health posts in the country.[77] Local and regional health facilities are often unable to assist landmine victims beyond bandaging wounds and preparing the victim for transport to the central hospital in Maputo or to military hospitals that have the only surgical facilities available in the country. These ill-equipped facilities are often unprepared for mine victims who, while representing only four percent of surgical admissions, use 25 percent of hospital resources.[78] Reaching health services may be an insurmountable task for many mine victims. Even where services are readily available and nearby, they may be inaccessible because there is no transportation or because access to such facilities is cutoff by mines. Casualties arriving in Maputo Central Hospital typically have traveled for two to four days, far in excess of the six-hour period after which the likelihood of infection or complications increases. Many landmine victims die of relatively minor wounds that become infected.

Projections of landmine victims in Mozambique range from 7000 to as many as 10,000 to 15,000.

ADEMIMO, the Association of Military Mozambican Handicapped, estimates that there are 7000 surviving mine victims in the military alone. These rates place Mozambique's average injury and death rate at .5 to 1 per 1,000. Statistics on mine casualties, however, are incomplete. They have been provided through hospitals, clinics and demining agencies, and probably over represent the numbers of soldiers and amputees who made it to medical or rehabilitation facilities. Using the conservative estimate of 7000 victims currently in the country, the economic burden represented by the direct costs their medical and rehabilitative care alone is $21 million.

Until 1990, the government did not permit records showing the type of device that caused war-related injuries of amputees or showing whether the victim was a civilian or soldier.[79] Information on mine accidents was sporadic and anecdotal; data collection depended on the presence of relief agencies or NGOs being in the right place at the right time. Mine incidents in areas under Renamo influence or in isolated districts have been largely unrecorded. Beginning in August 1993, a centralized database at the UN Mine Clearance Project was created to record mine incidents. The UN database recorded a total of 158 victims in 82 mine incidents in 1993 and the first six months of 1994. Twenty-nine percent of those recorded as involved in mine incidents died as a result of their injuries. Forty-three percent of incidents reported did not indicate the sex or age of the mine victim. For the remaining 90 cases where the information was provided, almost 79 percent were adult males, 14.4 percent were adult females, and 6.6 percent were children. The provinces most affected--or from which more reporting occurred--were Sofala, Manica and Maputo. But there is concern that conditions throughout the country are continuing to inhibit accurate reporting of landmine incidents.

The results of a 1994 study by Physicians for Human Rights (PHR) among 2568 individuals in Sofala province and 4677 individuals in Manica province show that these concerns are valid. The study identified 251 victims in 1033 households surveyed in the two provinces--or 16.7 landmine casualties per 1000 people. Almost 48 percent of landmine victims died as a result of their injuries. Seventy-seven percent of survivors underwent amputations; 88 percent of all amputations were to the lower-limb. Of the amputees identified in the study, 40 percent received a prosthesis and 87 percent used them. PHR found that sixty-eight percent of the victims were civilians and most were adult males. Women victims made up 16 percent of the total and seven percent were children under the age of 15. Most accidents occurred on a trail or working in the fields.

While male victims appear to far outnumber female victims, data collected in previous studies and rehabilitation facilities have shown divergent figures, with female victims ranging from 16 percent to 60 percent of the total.[80] Numbers of mine victims by province have also varied significantly: an ICRC clinic reported that most accidents occurred in Sofala and Manica provinces, while another study did not even mentioning Manica as a particular problem.[81]

Nearly six million Mozambicans of the total population of twelve million fled their homes at some point during the 1980s. At the time of the *Peace Agreement* in October 1992, between 1.3 to 2 million refugees were in five host countries and an additional 4.5 million were internally displaced. Most refugees came from rural areas and were subsistence farmers. Of the 1,261,200 refugees registered with the UNHCR at the time of the *Agreement*, 57.8 percent were from Tete Province and

17.7 percent from Zambezia Province. Most of the rest came from Niassa, Sofala, Manica, Gaza and Maputo provinces. Tete, Sofala and Manica provinces are considered to be severely mined. Zambezia and Gaza are heavily mined.

With the signing of the peace agreement, many began to return home and by the end of 1993, approximately 500,000 refugees were back in the country. One year later, the total of returnees was 1.6 million and in mid-1995, UNHCR reported that all Mozambicans were home. UNHCR, along with other UN agencies, NGOs and the government worked together to rehabilitate districts that were identified as priorities for refugee return in Tete, Manica, Zambezia, Sofala and Gaza provinces. In September and October 1993, in Tete province alone 15 people were injured and two were killed by landmines. Of these, eleven were men from the Malawian border camps who had returned to Mozambique to establish homes for their families. Many more incidents may occur as refugees resettle in areas that have been abandoned. Returnees counted as having returned spontaneously to Mozambique after the peace agreement are reported to have returned again to Malawi--after finding their home communities in Mozambique were heavily mined.

Mozambican refugees in Zimbabwe were also expected to face significant repatriation difficulties due to mines. About 50 percent of refugees in Zimbabwe originate from districts in Manica province and an additional 18 percent from one district (Changara) in Tete Province--districts known to be mined or were inaccessible at the time of the peace accord. About 90 percent of the refugees in Swaziland were expected to return to heavily-mined areas in Maputo Province. The remaining ten percent planned to return to areas in Gaza Province that were reported to be inaccessible.

IDPs have also experienced resettlement difficulties due to the presence of landmines in their communities. Since the peace agreement, 30 percent (about 1.5 million) of those reported to be internally displaced (particularly in the northern provinces of Tete and Zambezia), have returned to their home areas. Another three million, however, particularly those in the southern provinces, were inhibited from returning because of the threat of landmines.

III. The Enduring Legacy

Landmines have been called a poor man's weapon. They are cheap, easy to obtain, and easy to use. They are the weapon-of-choice for fighting forces with limited resources. But landmines also have a disproportionate impact on the poor and on the world's poorest societies. The majority of countries contaminated by landmines are countries with the least resources available to contend with their costs. Despite the increasing recognition of the immediate and long-term consequences of landmine proliferation, more landmines continue to be sown than are being cleared. The United Nations estimates that, in 1993, approximately two million new landmines were laid. During that same period only 100,000 landmines were lifted--at a cost of $70 million. This discrepancy created a "clearance deficit" of 1.9 million landmines, and added $1.4 billion to the cost of clearing the world of landmines.[82] At the current rate of mines sown to mines lifted, two decades will be added to the amount of time it will take to demine contaminated countries.[83]

Nevertheless, mines continue to be produced, sold, exported, traded, and sown. Most of the mines found in contaminated countries are not made by them. Eighty-five percent of mines cleared in affected countries were purchased or transferred from producer countries.[84] Of the more than 255 million landmines manufactured over the past 25 years, 190 million have been antipersonnel mines. At one time or another, at least 100 companies have been involved in the production of 360 types of antipersonnel mines in 55 countries. Current production stands at approximately five million mines each year. (That figure is down from an average of 10 million mines produced in each of the last 25 years.) Of the $20 billion annual global arms trade, it is estimated that the value of conventional antipersonnel mines produced is less than $100 million.[85]

China, the former Soviet Union and Italy[86] have been the major producers and traders of landmines in recent years. Other landmine manufacturers have included the former Czechoslovakia and former Yugoslavia--along with Egypt, Pakistan and South Africa. Prior to the mid-1980s, the United Kingdom, Belgium and the United States ranked among the world's top producers and exporters of landmines. Other significant exporters in that period included Bulgaria, France and Hungary.[87]

Recent steps taken to control the export of landmines will not, by themselves, adequately address the problem of landmine production and deployment.[88] The problem of landmines and their long-term impact on society, as clearly shown in the countries researched for this report, cannot be solved through limited arms control measures. This report shows that landmines are indiscriminate weapons that target civilian populations, and that their impact on those civilian populations is not proportionate to their military utility.

A writer from the U.S. Army School of the Americas at Fort Benning, Georgia, recently posed the following questions: "What crop costs a hundred times more to reap than to plant and has no market value when harvested? What weapon is still lethal to unsuspecting human targets when the soldiers who brought it to the battlefield have become old men? What Cold War legacy has the greatest mathematical probability of claiming victims now and for the next couple of generations? What weapon employed by US forces under scrupulous adherence to the laws of land warfare may have inflicted more friendly than enemy casualties in several campaigns?"[89]

The answer, of course, is antipersonnel landmines. Because the consequences of landmine use are not conflict-limited, societies are affected by landmines for generations. Landmines are not simply a momentary crisis for a country in conflict--they are a long-term impediment to complete peace and post-conflict redevelopment. People now living with landmines are significantly affected by their use. But so are their children. And their children's children.

International law requires that this impact be given equal weight to military utility when determining the legality of the use of a weapon. The growing body of research on the impact of landmines is clear evidence that their cost outweighs their immediate utility. Yet the military remains reluctant to address collateral damage over the life-cycle of the weapon. It is likely that the underlying concern is not the antipersonnel landmine itself, but possible repercussions that could affect a wide array of conventional weapons. In 1994, after legislation was introduced in the U.S. Senate that would have placed a one-year moratorium on the production and procurement of landmines, the U.S. military made its concern clear. In stating opposition to the proposed bill, the Chief of Staff of the U.S. Army wrote that "the precedent established--that of unilateral denial to U.S. forces of a legitimate, essential weapon based on potential post-conflict humanitarian concerns--threatens the use of a wide range of military weapons."[90]

This report demonstrates that the post-conflict humanitarian cost of continued landmine use is not a "potential concern" but a social and economic disaster for the millions of people affected by their use around the world.

Jody Williams
Brattleboro, Vermont

Shawn Roberts
San Francisco, California

August, 1995

Part Two

Severely Mined Countries

BACKGROUND INFORMATION ON AFGHANISTAN

General Background. Afghanistan covers a total area of 652,000 sq km. It is an extremely poor, landlocked country bordered by Iran, Pakistan, China, and the former Soviet republics of Tajikistan, Uzbekistan and Turkmenistan. It is highly dependent on farming (wheat especially) and livestock raising (primarily cattle, sheep and goats). The territory is divided into 29 provinces, and further into 356 districts.

Mined Areas. 4235 minefields have been identified in Afghanistan, in 27 of the country's 29 provinces. The total mined area in the country has been identified as covering 488.9 sq km.

Population. Afghanistan has an estimated total population of 17,419,811. An estimated 450,000 individuals are internally displaced within Afghanistan (nearly 300,000 of whom are living in refugee camps and some 150,000 of whom are living with relatives or in rental units around Jalalabad). Another 2.8 million Afghans remain outside the country as refugees in Pakistan and Iran. These population figures include an estimated 1.5 million *kuchi* nomads, of whom approximately one-third fled the country as refugees.

Ethnicity. The country is ethnically diverse, featuring Pashtun, Tajik, Uzbek, Hazara and at least nineteen other ethnic groups.

Languages. There are four major language groups (Pashtu, Afghan Persian/Dari and Turkic languages including Uzbez and Turkmen) and thirty minor language groups.

Literacy. Twenty-nine percent of the population age 15 and over is literate (44 percent of males, 14 percent of females).

Religions. The majority of the population is Sunni Muslim. A significant minority is Shiite Muslim, and a small number follow other religions.

Political Divisions. There are four main political groupings in the country: the Rabani alliance (consisting of the Jamait-I-Islami of President Rabani and his military commander Afmad Shah Masood, the Ittehad-i-Islami and the Harakat-i-Islami), the Taliban (the recently emerging force composed of religious students), the Supreme Coordination Council/Shoria Hamahangi (consisting of the Hezb-i-Islami of former Afghan premier Gulbuddin Hekmatyar, the Afghan National Liberation Front led by former Afghan president Sibghatullah Majaddedi, the Junbish-i-Mili Islami of General Dostam, and the Hezb-i-Wahdat of the late Shiite leader Abdul Ali Mazari, who was recently killed by the Taliban), and the neutral parties not involved in the fighting (consisting of the Hezb-i-Islami, the National Islamic Front of Afghanistan, and the Harakat-i-Inqilab Islami).

Rural v. Urban. More than four-fifths of Afghanistan's population is rural, and nearly eight percent of the country's population is nomadic. Nomads (*kuchis*) have a traditional pattern of summer grazing in the mountains and winter in the warmer lowlands, including in Pakistan and Iran. Traditionally, the highest density population in Afghanistan was centered in Kabul and in a band running from the northern provinces south-east to Nangarhar. The conflict in Kabul has shifted this pattern somewhat, with many of its inhabitants now living in Jalalabad or elsewhere.

Arable Land. The Afghan people, land and economy are mainly agricultural, and the small amount of industrial development is linked to the processing of agricultural commodities or the manufacture of farm inputs. Much of the country is too steep for cultivation or is dry desert. Only 7.6 million hectares (an estimated 12-13 percent of the total land surface) is arable. About half of this land was cultivated in pre-war years because of unreliable water supplies, with the other half lying fallow. Of the land cultivated, about two thirds (5.2 million hectares) was irrigated; another 2.4 million hectares were rain-fed. Irrigated land accounted for the greatest part of production. Irrigation of flat land is limited by the amount of water available from melting snow, rivers, wells or spring-fed *karez* (underground tunnels). Prior to the war, about 85 percent of the population lived in the country, and much of the other 15 percent still owned land.

Natural Resources. Afghanistan has one of the largest iron ore and copper deposits in the world, and has substantial unexploited natural gas and oil reserves. The country is also endowed with a variety of semi-precious stones.

Geography. Afghanistan has three distinctive regions. The northern Plains is the major agricultural area. The southwestern Plateau consists primarily of lowlands, desert and semidesert landscape and includes the Rigestan desert. These regions are separated by the Central Highlands. Arid rangeland and a small amount of good pasture occupy almost half of Afghanistan's total land area.

The Economy. Afghanistan has a developing economy that is based largely on subsistence-level agricultural production. The gross domestic product (GDP) of $200 per capita is among the lowest in the world (1989 est.). The GDP originates primarily in agricultural output (about two-thirds of the total), followed by the combined category of mining, manufacturing, and public utilities, and then by trade.

AFGHANISTAN

Part I: Introduction

Afghanistan, located in northwest Asia, is bordered by Iran, Pakistan, China and the former Soviet republics of Tajikistan, Uzbekistan and Turkmenistan. Slightly smaller than the state of Texas--or about twice the size of Poland--it is a landlocked country and is dependent on its neighbors for access to international markets.

The conflict of the last two decades has had devastating consequences--an estimated nine percent of the population has been killed, and tens of thousands disabled. More than one-third of the population has been displaced, either inside the country or to Pakistan and Iran. An estimated 50 percent of Afghanistan's villages have been destroyed. Twenty-five percent of the paved roads, 33 percent of the secondary roads, and approximately 300 bridges have been damaged or destroyed.[1] The disruption of the country's agricultural base has left the population highly dependant on food aid for survival.

Afghanistan is one of the world's least developed countries. It is ranked 171st of 173 countries listed in the United Nations Development Programme's *Human Development Report 1994*. In areas of maternal and infant mortality, health, water supply and sanitation and education, Afghanistan ranks as one of the most impoverished nations in the world.

Afghanistan is also one of the most heavily mined nations in the world. Projections based on information obtained from the communist Najibullah regime, and reports from the former Soviet Union and the *mujahedeen* (holy warriors), show that ten million landmines contaminate the country. In effect, all of Afghanistan is a minefield: nearly all of the national infrastructure has been mined, as well as much of the arable and grazing land. Most demining experts agree, however, that the quantity of mines in a given area is largely irrelevant: the important issue is the area of land made unusable or unproductive due to the presence of mines. Removing the mines costs millions of dollars each year. Thousands of Afghans have been maimed and killed by mines and refugees have been inhibited from returning to their homes to rebuild their lives.

Background on the War and Peace Accords

Afghanistan has suffered political turmoil since King Zahir Shah was overthrown by his cousin, Mohammed Daoud, in 1973. Political inaction by the Zahir government, coupled with its failure to meet basic needs, helped to create the conditions for the coup. A drought in 1971 and 1972 reduced food production by 20 percent, and numbers of livestock by 40 percent. Corruption and mismanagement prevented sufficient distribution of food aid. An estimated 500,000 Afghans died in the resulting famine.[2]

Mohammed Daoud's government gained initial support from the Soviet Union, but after growing concern with increasing dependence, Daoud purged Communists from his government and the army. The result was the Saur Coup of 1978 and Daoud's assassination. The new government issued *Basic Lines of Revolutionary Duties of Government of Democratic Afghanistan*, its platform for reforming Afghan society. Poorly implemented, highly ideological attempts at social change--including programs to redistribute land, abolish usurious land-related debt and bride prices, and launch a literacy campaign (especially for women)--clashed with the society's long-standing cultural beliefs and alienated the Afghan people. Religious leaders declared a *jihad* (holy war), and men throughout the country took up arms as *mujahedeen*. Armed rebellion grew and population movement to urban centers and outside the country began.

Factional divisions within the government increased along with its inability to control the escalating conflict. These tensions led to the invasion of Afghanistan by the Soviet army on Christmas Eve of 1979. Along with Soviet intervention came massive infusions of high-tech military equipment, including jet aircraft and helicopter gunships--and landmines. Over time, the *mujahedeen* acquired high technology equipment from the United States, China, Arab nations and other sources. The destructive capacity of the war significantly increased.[3]

When Mikhail Gorbachev came to power in the Soviet Union in 1986, his commitment to ending Soviet involvement in Afghanistan mirrored Soviet disillusionment with the prolonged conflict. In 1987, Soviet-backed President Mohammed Najibullah (the fourth president since the Saur Coup) announced a ceasefire and initiated a policy of national reconciliation. While the ceasefire did not hold, these reconciliation policies brought change: amnesty for some of the regime's opponents, an invitation of return to refugees, and the beginning of political links with tribal leaders.

By April 1988, UN-sponsored negotiations to end the fighting resulted in an agreement calling on Soviet troops to withdraw from Afghanistan by February 15, 1989. Afghanistan and Pakistan signed a treaty to this effect (the *Accords*) with the United States and Soviet Union named as guarantors.[4] The *Accords* increased pressure on Afghanistan's political parties in Pakistan and Iran to form an alternative government. Seven Sunni parties formed an Afghan Interim Government based in Peshawar, but it was not effective. Shiite parties in Iran joined in the Alliance of Eight, which was also plagued by rivalries.[5]

Although the Soviet withdrawal took place as scheduled, the *Accords* failed to bring about a political settlement agreeable to a majority of Afghans. Fighting intensified and finally, in April 1992, the Najibullah government fell and Kabul was occupied by the *mujahedeen*--who established the Islamic State of Afghanistan. However, the collapse of the Najibullah government did not bring peace. The resistance parties formed an interim government, with Burnahuddin Rabani as president, but the country is now plagued by civil war brought on by factional fighting. Kabul has become the central point in the struggle for power.[6]

In late 1994 a new Afghan fighting force known as the *Taliban* began an offensive in Kandahar (Afghanistan's second largest city). The *Taliban* sprang up when students at Muslim religious schools banded together "to rid Afghanistan of the armed factions that had divided the country into fiefs and preyed on Afghans."

By February 1995, *Taliban* units had taken control of nearly one-third of the country, had dislodged the Hezb-I-Islami faction of former premier Gulbuddin Hekmatyar from around Kabul, and had taken up its own positions on the outskirts of the city in preparation for an assault against forces loyal to the Rabani government.[7] The *Taliban* also began an offensive in western Afghanistan, engaging in heavy fighting around the city of Herat against forces loyal to Rabani. By March 19, government forces defeated the *Taliban* in Kabul, but the Herat conflict continued into April.

Prior to the *Taliban* assaults, President Rabani agreed to cede power in February 1995 to a transitional governing council--proposed by the United Nations through its representative to Afghanistan, Mahmoud Mestiri. The transitional governing council was to be made up of representatives of the eight *mujahedeen* groups that participated in the anti-Soviet resistance, of five regional groups (which have established power in key provincial cities, including Jalalabad, Mazar-I-Sharif and Herat), and of a number of prominent Afghan personalities who have played no part in the fighting that has ravaged the country for the past 16 years. Prospects for peace are now thought to rest with the Rabani government and with the *Taliban*, with a significant role to be played by the Shoria Hamahangi opposition coalition (especially the Hezb-I-Islami led by former premier Hekmatyar and the Afghan Liberation Front of former president Sibghatullah Mojaddedi).

The Use of Mines in the Afghan War

Estimates of the number of mines used in the Afghan war vary. The total number of mines now contaminating Afghan territory is thought to be around ten million.[8] All sides in the conflict used mines, but the vast majority were laid by former Soviet or regime forces. Most of the antipersonnel mines were deployed by former Soviet or regime troops, while the majority of antitank mines were deployed by

the *mujahedeen*.

Regime forces made extensive use of protective minefields around garrisons, posts and vital assets, particularly around the major cities close to the Iranian and Pakistani borders (such as Herat, Kandahar, Jalalabad and Khost). The same tactic was followed in strategic locations outside the cities, at airports, government installations and power stations. Possible *mujahedeen* infiltration routes and partly destroyed buildings were often mined.

The former Soviet Union engaged in the indiscriminate use of scatterable "butterfly-type" mines[9] that were frequently dropped on mountain passes, villages and enemy bases. Demining teams have also found that Soviet and regime forces laid booby-trapped mines. Mines were used to depopulate towns, restrict the movement of people, and disrupt agriculture in order to weaken support for the *mujahedeen*. The *mujahedeen* used far fewer mines against the Soviet and regime forces-- mainly to block roads and tracks.

Factions involved in the internal conflict since the Soviet withdrawal and the fall of the Najibullah regime have also laid mines: the Hezb-I-Wahdat planted mines in western Kabul which have resulted in an average of six injuries per day since early 1995.[10] Demining officials also suspect that new mines were laid in Baghlan province during fighting in early 1994.

The United Nations Office for the Coordination of Humanitarian Assistance to Afghanistan (UNOCHA), which coordinates the demining program, reports that some mine fields laid by Soviet and Afghan government forces were recorded and catalogued according to military procedures. This was not the case with most of the mines laid by the *mujahedeen*, which were typically laid in unconventional and unpredictable patterns.[11] The records that exist are useless. The usefulness of any such records was lost as many areas were fought over, mined and remined, and won and lost by both sides during the war. Consequently, many areas that were once mapped may now have mines laid in a combination of random and organized patterns. Other factors such as rain and flooding sometimes change the location of mines. Additionally, as many of the mines were delivered by aircraft, their remote delivery precluded accurate or meaningful recording.[12] Due to these factors, minefield records may only be used to check unsurveyed areas for the likelihood of mines.

Mines have been found in a wide variety of locations in Afghanistan. Although mines are traditionally used to protect a specific area or deny access to a militarily valuable position, in Afghanistan they were also frequently used as a form of civilian harassment. Commonly mined locations included residential areas, agricultural and grazing land, irrigation canals and roads. Mines are most often found in the following areas in Afghanistan:

Types of Antipersonnel Landmines Found in Afghanistan	
PMN; PMN-2	Ex-USSR
POMZ; POMZ-2; POMZ-2M	Ex-USSR
PMD-6; PMD-6M	Ex-USSR
PFM-1; PFM-1S	Ex-USSR
PMN-2	Ex-USSR
PGMDM	Ex-USSR
OZM-3; OZM-72; OZM-4	Ex-USSR
MC-3	Ex-USSR
MON-50; MON-90; MON-100; MON-200	Ex-USSR
PMP	Ex-USSR
POM-2S	Ex-USSR
VP-12; VP-13	Ex-USSR
PP-MI-SR	Ex-Czech.
PP-MI-SR II	Ex-Czech.
M18A1	US
Type 72; Type 69	China
SB-33; VS-50	Italy

[Sources: Mine Clearance Planning Agency; Human Rights Watch Arms Project.]

--Along unused footpaths or tracks,
--On unused roadways,
--On the verges of tracks and roadways,
--In vehicle turn-around points,
--Near culverts and bridge abutments,
--Along damaged building walls
--In doorways and rooms of deserted houses,
--In and around wells or water access points,
--Around military posts and destroyed,
--On or near destroyed vehicles,
--In areas where people might hide.[13]

Part II: Landmines and the Disruption of the Infrastructure

The widespread use of landmines in Afghanistan affected transportation, crop production, livestock, water supply and energy generation and distribution.

Preferred locations for mining included villages, fields, tracks, roads, bridges and water sources. Even shrines and historic landmarks have been mined.[14] UNOCHA notes that in some regions, mines are found nearly everywhere, while in other regions a few mines deny the use of vast areas of land.[15] Although mines affect the entire nation, the provinces bordering Iran and Pakistan (the western, southern and eastern sections of the country) are the most heavily mined. The problem of landmines is so extensive that until mines are cleared from the priority areas (which is expected to take until at least the end of 1997), major rehabilitation or reconstruction activities cannot be undertaken.[16]

Agriculture

At the time of the Soviet invasion in 1979, an estimated 85 percent of the country's 15 million people lived in 22,000 villages.[17] The number of villages inhabited in 1994 was 19,924.[18] The rural population was engaged in dry farming, irrigated farming, animal husbandry, the production of food crops and a variety of fruits.

Prior to the outbreak of civil war, Afghanistan achieved self-sufficiency in wheat.[19] Per capita consumption was among the highest in the world (180 kg/year). Seventy-seven percent of all wheat and 85 percent of all food and agricultural crops were grown on irrigated land supported by an extensive network of traditional underground tunnels (*karez*). Other cereal crops included maize, barley, and rice. Industrial and cash crops included cotton, sugar beet, oilseeds, fruits and vegetables. Livestock production was an integral part of farming.[20]

Production Losses Related to War

The war caused major damage to the productive capacity of the agrarian economy. Irrigation canals were mined or bombed, thousands of villages were destroyed, and more than 50 percent of the estimated 20 million livestock were killed. Between 1978 and 1986, production declines of 33 percent and 50 percent, respectively, for irrigated and dry land wheat crops were reported-- suggesting a drop in production to 45 percent of 1978 levels. Gradual increases in production have been recorded since 1988, resulting in production equaling 60 percent of pre-war totals. Production levels were sufficient, however, to meet the needs of only two-thirds of the population, clearly indicating a need for continued imports of cereals and other food.[21]

A policy of depopulating the rural areas of Afghanistan was followed during the war, in order to deny the *mujahedeen* local support. This policy involved the indiscriminate mining and bombing of villages and farmlands, thereby denying the rural population a means of making a living.[22] As a result, an estimated two million farmers left their lands,[23] many becoming refugees in Pakistan or Iran, or internal refugees who migrated to overcrowded cities. No longer able to engage in traditional patterns of production, those displaced by mines have become an economic burden. This displacement has led to a decrease in food production and an increase in the inflation rate for food and fuel--of some 200 to 300 percent.[24]

Reduced Cultivation and Access to Water

Although it is nearly impossible to determine the extent to which decreases in agricultural production are due to the presence of landmines (rather than lack of farm inputs, fertilizer and farm labor), VVAF obtained important information regarding reduced land cultivation and the impact of mines on traditional activities at the household level. VVAF administered an extensive landmine survey among 4990 households in Afghan villages (representing 38,492 individuals in six provinces of the country), 2277 households in refugee camps in both Pakistan and in Afghanistan (representing 16,729 individuals), and among 1432 *kuchi* families (representing 11,381 individuals in settlement sites in Nangarhar, Herat and Khost).

The survey was undertaken with logistical assistance provided by the Mine Clearance Planning Agency (MCPA) and financial support from UNOCHA, UNHCR, UNICEF and the FAO. Survey design and training was provided by Barbara Reed, a consultant to CIET international and VVAF.

Forty-three percent of those families surveyed reported that they would cultivate more land, if it were not for the presence of landmines. The total land that could be cultivated in the village areas surveyed was equal to 150 percent of the areas currently under cultivation. Fifty-five percent of the village families surveyed were cultivating land (an average of 2.71 *jeribs* per household including those not cultivating land, or 4.96 *jeribs* if only those cultivating are included in the average).[25]

Each family that responded that mines were preventing them from cultivating some land were asked how the mines were keeping them from doing so. Four types of responses were received: there were mines on the land, mines were along or near irrigation canals preventing their maintenance and repair (and thereby preventing irrigation), mines surrounded a water source, or mines blocked land access. Mines on the land were the primary means of preventing cultivation (80 percent of responses), in each survey area and in most villages. Mines preventing irrigation was the second largest response overall (16 percent). The distribution of responses received from households regarding the ways mines prevent cultivation is presented in Table A-1:

Table A-1 **Ways that Mines Prevent Cultivation**

	Nangarhar	Khost	Northern Provinces	Herat	Total
Land is mined	98	93	58	81	80
Mines prevent irrigation	2	6	32	18	16
Mines block water source	<1	1	3	0	1
Mines block access to land	0	0	7	0	2

Table A-2 summarizes information provided about land cultivated at the time of the survey by the households interviewed, the amount of additional land that the households would cultivate if there were no landmines, the sum of the land cultivated, and the amount a family would like to cultivate--but cannot--because of mines.

Table A-2   Cultivable land: in use or prevented from use by mines

	Nangarhar	Khost	Northern	Herat	Total
A: % HH Cultivating	42	72	47	50	55
B: *Jerib* land farmed	2,600	3,463	4,395	3,065	13,523
C: Avg plot size (*jerib*) (incl 0/excl 0)	1.08/4.30	2.70/3.75	3.93/8.29	2.30/4.59	2.71/4.96
D: % HH mines prevent farm	43	57	46	27	43
E: % HH would farm	49	77	57	56	60
F: *Jerib* land mine-blocked	3,212	6,910	7,389	2,720	20,231
G: Avg plot size added if no mines (*jerib*) (incl 0/excl 0)	2.56/5.97	5.39/9.45	6.62/14.43	2.04/7.64	4.06/8.41
H: *Jerib* land would farm (current + blocked)	5,812	10,383	11,784	5,775	33,754
I: Avg plot size desired (*jerib*) (incl 0/ excl 0)	4.64/9.41	8.11/10.47	10.56/18.60	4.34/7.75	6.77/11.27

The rows of the table correspond by letter to:

A: The percentage of families interviewed that had some amount of land under cultivation.

B: The total amount of land cultivated by all of the families responding from the province, in *jerib*.

C: Average household plot sizes calculated two ways: The total amount of land (from B) divided by the total number of households interviewed/ The total amount of land divided by the number of households with some land under cultivation at time of the survey. (*Jerib*)

D: The percentage of households that said that if there were no landmines they would cultivate additional land.

E: The percentage of families that were either cultivating land at the time of the survey and/or said that if there were no mines they would cultivate some land

F: The total sum of additional lands that the households said they would cultivate if there were no mines. (*Jerib*)

G: This is the average household plot of additional land that would be cultivated if not for mines, calculated two ways: The total of additional land (F) divided by the total number of households interviewed/ The total of additional land divided by the number of households responding that they would cultivate more if not for mines (number represented in percentage in D). (*Jerib*)

H: The total amount of land either under cultivation at the time of the survey plus the amount that total that the households would cultivate if there were no mines (B + F). (*Jerib*)

I: The average plot size that was being cultivated or would be cultivated if there were no mines calculated two ways: The total amount of land cultivated or that would be cultivated (H) divided by the total number of households/The total amount of land cultivated or that would be cultivated (H) divided by the total number of households already cultivating or which would cultivate if there were no mines (represented by E). (*Jerib*)

Irrigation

As reflected in our survey results, water supplies and irrigation systems throughout Afghanistan were extensively mined. This mining has had a significant social and economic impact--especially in desert areas. Some *karez* (traditional underground water storage tanks) and canals were affected by mines, although not as extensively as initially feared. Once destroyed or encircled by mines, water sources and irrigation systems are not easily repaired. Their loss can ruin the economy of a village.[26] Not only does their loss deprive local populations of water needed for crops, many injuries and deaths result among civilians who seek access to water for themselves or their livestock.[27] Although irrigated farmland constitutes only 20 percent of the total area affected by landmines, such areas provide three-fourths of Afghanistan's total wheat production and an estimated 85 percent of all food and agricultural crops.[28]

Livestock Production

In Afghanistan, livestock has historically been a major part of agricultural production and has made up the bulk of capital assets. Livestock is the economic underpinning and a key indicator of wealth, particularly for the nomad economy. Once destroyed, herds take years to replace.

Although it is impossible to determine exactly how many animals have been killed due to mines since the start of the war, village-level households, refugee and displaced families, and *kuchi*s surveyed by VVAF report significant livestock losses due to mines: 34 percent of the village (non-nomad) families surveyed lost at least one animal to landmines. A total of 40,039 animals were killed among the village households alone--23,308 sheep, 8305 goats, 2674 donkeys, 259 camels, 5104 cattle, and 389 horses. Sixty-one percent of these (non-nomad) families owned animals. The animals killed by mines represent approximately 47 percent of the current flocks owned by the village families.

Among refugee and displaced families, 11 percent lost one or more animals in mine incidents, with a total of 1130 animals lost. The largest percentage of families affected (38 percent) was in Pakistan. Animal losses among families in Pakistan were equal in number to approximately one-half of the number of animals currently owned. Among the families in Samar Khel Camp in Nangarhar, 17 percent were affected, with an average of 11.3 animals reported lost per family.

Due to the particular circumstances of the nomadic populations in Afghanistan, which have traditionally been involved in herding, VVAF separately administered and analyzed its landmine survey among 1432 nomad (*kuchi*) families (580 in Nangarhar, 597 in Herat, and 255 in Khost), representing 11,381 individuals. The following data were obtained from surveys administered among those nomad (*kuchi*) families:

--65 percent of all nomad families reported having lost at least one animal to landmines (Nangarhar 55 percent, Herat 71 percent, Khost 73 percent). Eighty-four percent of nomad families currently own animals (76 percent in Nangarhar, 93 percent in Herat and 80 percent in Khost). The number of animals killed by landmines is equal to 60 percent of the current flocks owned by these families.